Assessing
the Environmental Impact
of Farm Policies

T0273246

AEI STUDIES IN AGRICULTURAL POLICY

Assessing
the Environmental Impact
of Farm Policies

Walter N. Thurman

The AEI Press

Publisher for the American Enterprise Institute

WASHINGTON, D. C.

1995

Distributed to the Trade by National Book Network, 15200 NBN Way, Blue Ridge Summit, PA 17214. To order call toll free 1-800-462-6420 or 1-717-794-3800. For all other inquiries please contact the AEI Press, 1150 Seventeenth Street, N.W., Washington, D.C. 20036 or call 1-800-862-5801.

Library of Congress Cataloging-in-Publication Data

Thurman, Walter N.
    Assessing the environmental impact of farm policies / Walter N. Thurman.
        p. cm. — (AEI studies in agricultural policy)
    Includes bibliographical references.
    ISBN 0-8447-3915-4 (paper : alk. paper)
    I.   II. Title. III. Series.
HG9968.G66   1995
368.1'2—dc20   95-16099
                                       CIP

1 3 5 7 9 10 8 6 4 2

The AEI Press
Publisher for the American Enterprise Institute
1150 17th Street, N.W., Washington, D.C. 20036

Contents

CONTENTS

Foreword

Assessing the Environmental Impact of Farm Policies, by Walter N. Thurman, is one of eight in a series devoted to agricultural policy reform published by the American Enterprise Institute. AEI has a long tradition of contributing to the effort to understand and improve agricultural policy. AEI published books of essays before the 1977, 1981, and 1985 farm bills.

Agricultural policy has increasingly become part of the general policy debate. Whether the topic is trade policy as in the North American Free Trade Agreement and the General Agreement on Tariffs and Trade or budget deficit issues such as farm subsidy entitlements, the same forces that affect other government programs are shaping farm policy discussions. It is fitting then that the AEI Studies in Agricultural Policy deal with these issues with the same tools and approaches applied to other economic and social topics.

Periodic farm bills (along with budget acts) remain the principal vehicles for policy changes related to agriculture, food, and other rural issues. The 1990 farm legislation expires in 1995, and in recognition of the opportunity presented by the national debate surrounding the 1995 farm bill, the American Enterprise Institute has launched a major research project. With the new farm bill, policy makers have an opportunity to bring agriculture more in line with market realities. The AEI studies were intended to capitalize on the current opportunity to create better public policy.

The AEI project includes research studies on eight

related topics prepared by recognized experts and scholars. Each study investigates the public rationale for government's role with respect to several agricultural issues. The authors have developed evidence on the effects of recent policies and analyzed alternatives. Most research was carried out in 1994, and draft reports were discussed at a policy research workshop held in Washington, D.C., November 3–4, 1994.

The individual topics include investigation of:

- the rationale for and consequences of farm programs in general
- specific reforms of current farm programs appropriate for 1995, including analysis of individual programs for grains, milk, cotton, and sugar, among others
- agricultural trade policy for commodities in the context of recent multilateral trade agreements, with attention both to long-run goals of free trade and to intermediate steps
- crop insurance and disaster aid policy
- the government's role in conservation of natural resources and the environmental consequences of farm programs
- farm credit policy, including analysis of both subsidy and regulation
- food safety policy
- the role of public R&D policy for agriculture, what parts of the research portfolio should be subsidized, and how the payoff to publicly supported science can be improved through better policy

Although conservation programs in agriculture have been with us for sixty years, they have been growing rapidly over the past decade. Walter Thurman looks at the rationale and effects of farm programs designed to produce environmental benefits. He shows that some programs have been inappropriately targeted toward reducing costs that are private rather than public and for which individual farmers have incentives to use resources wisely. For other programs, Thurman asks if they have achieved their aims and how costly they have been relative to alternatives and relative to the benefits achieved. Thurman also investigates the resource and conservation effects of farm programs designed for other purposes. He shows how program reforms have reduced negative environmental consequences, but how even less environmental damage is threatened by further reducing program-created incentives for farm-specific crop choices.

Selected government policy may be helpful in allowing agriculture to become more efficient and effective. Unfortunately, most agricultural policy in the United States fails in that respect. In many ways, the policies of the past six decades have been counterproductive and counter to productivity. Now, in the final few years of the twentieth century, flaws in policies developed decades ago are finally becoming so obvious that farm policy observers and participants are willing to consider even eliminating many traditional subsidies and regulations. In the current context, another round of minor fixes is now seen as insufficient.

In 1995, Congress seems ready to ask tough questions about agricultural policy. How much reform is forthcoming, however, and which specific changes will be accomplished are not settled and depend on the information and analysis available to help guide the process. Understanding the consequences of alternative public policies is important. The AEI Studies in Agricultural Policy are designed to aid the process now and for the future by improving the knowledge base on which public policy is built.

CHRISTOPHER DEMUTH
American Enterprise Institute
for Public Policy Research

1
Introduction

The effects of agriculture on the environment are increasingly found near the center of environmental concern. Public discussion preparatory to the 1995 farm bill makes it clear that environmental interests view the sixty-year-old farm programs as central to their agenda, both because they believe that farm programs have systematic and bad environmental results and because the farm bill provides a legislative opportunity for creating new regulation.[1] At a time when creative energy is being applied to redirecting farm programs toward environmental objectives, it is useful to assess the bias of the current programs. To begin, let us delimit the proper scope of public policy toward agricultural environmental problems.

The environmental effects of agriculture are real, and they are significant. They are also site specific, difficult to measure in any particular instance, and even more diffi-

---

1. Kenneth A. Cook, president of the Environmental Working Group: "Environmentalists have as much at stake in the next farm bill as we have in any other major environmental law" (*Progressive Farmer*, June 1994). Cook is described by *Progressive Farmer* as an early advocate of tying environmental regulations to farm program payments, as is accomplished by the conservation compliance provision of the 1985 Food Security Act.

cult to summarize in aggregate.[2] Further, and logically distinct, public policy should concern itself with some environmental effects but not others. When crop production leads to fertilizer runoff that overnourishes natural waterways and farmers do not bear the costs of the environmental damage, then society should pay attention, and government action may be beneficial. There are, however, environmental effects of agricultural production that are not externalities.

Where Are the Externalities?

When a landowner decides to farm in a way that erodes his soil but the erosion has no downstream external effects, then costs and benefits are both focused on the decision maker: there is no externality. Individuals may wish to convince the farmer that he is foolish to give the future productivity of his soil so little weight in his decision. But apart from, perhaps, educating the farmer about the value of his soil and the proper way to discount benefits and costs, the government has no obvious role to play.[3]

Externalities are potentially wealth-increasing transactions that do not occur. Parties who could mutually gain from exchange do not because they are separated by transactions costs. The downstream water users affected by

---

2. Smith (1992) heroically makes, to this author's knowledge, the only published attempt to calculate the total external environmental cost of U.S. crop production. Drawing from a variety of sources, he concludes that "including the instream effects of soil erosion, wetlands conversion, and groundwater contamination, agriculture's crop-related activities yield environmental cost estimates that range from less than one percent to over 40 percent of the value of crops produced per acre on the land deemed responsible for these impacts" (p. 1077).

3. As an empirical proposition, it is not at all clear that landowners neglect the value of their soil in making farming decisions. Miranowski and Hammes (1984) provide evidence that land markets reflect both the value of topsoil and the erosivity of particular fields.

agricultural runoff may be numerous and diverse, and the relationship between their water quality and the farming practices upstream may be dimly understood. The collective action problems faced by the numerous water users are one source of high transactions costs, which, in turn, are due to the absence of clear property rights. The difficulties in understanding the physical nature of the runoff problem are another source of transactions costs. Those thinking about government policy should keep in mind that the transactions costs that give rise to the externality do not disappear when the government addresses those externalities. The same transactions costs that prove problematic for the private resolution of environmental externalities often prove problematic for the effective implementation of environmental policy. Thus while the existence of an externality is a prerequisite for governmental redress of environmental harm, alone it does not justify government action.

What, then, are the external effects of agricultural production on the environment? Have they become worse in the recent past? The land base employed in U.S. agricultural production has remained roughly the same size over the past forty years. Production of crops and animal products has increased dramatically over the period, and farm labor has fallen by a factor of three (see Miranowski, Hrubovcak, and Sutton 1991). The increase in production resulted from a substitution away from labor and land and toward other inputs, primarily fertilizers and pesticides and, in the case of livestock, intensification of production on smaller acreage. Input substitution has taken place against a backdrop of constantly improving technical possibilities.

Any rise in the external environmental effects of U.S. agriculture in the aggregate, then, is not due to a larger geographic scale for agricultural production. Such increases result from the input substitution described. In-

3

creased use of fertilizers leads to runoff from fields that encourages the growth of algae and other plants and results in eutrophication of waterways. Increased use of pesticides can also lead to contaminated runoff, affecting drinking water or poisoning wildlife. Intensification of production on smaller acreage can increase soil erosion, which can itself impair water quality off site and also carry fertilizer and pesticide residue with it. In the case of animal production, the concentration of cattle and poultry operations can raise effluent above the assimilative capacity of the nearby environment. Each of these conditions is an instance of possible externality from agricultural production.

But the externalities just listed result from the interaction among parties and do not exist in isolation. Without downstream water users, the silting of waterways creates no externality. The reciprocal nature of externality has been stressed by writers following Coase (1960). In the present instance, the Coase tradition would argue that those negatively affected by agricultural operations are as responsible for the externality as the on-farm generators of the harm.

In fact, growth on the recipient side of environmental externalities is probably responsible for much of the increased concern over the environmental effects of agriculture. Several factors are involved in the off-farm growth of agricultural externalities. First, demand for recreational use of land has risen in recent decades and has heightened demand for land near agricultural operations. Agricultural runoff and its related problems can impair the value of recreational land use. Second, growth of suburban land uses into areas that were primarily agricultural has increased the value of clean water sources. The costs of chemical contamination of groundwater, therefore, have risen. Third, the demand for environmental quality appears to be highly income elastic, and the quantity demanded has grown along with U.S. per capita income.

4

What are the nonexternal environmental effects of agriculture—the ones more properly handled by private transaction than public coercion? The externalities mentioned do not exhaust the list of activities that take place on a farm that influence environmental quality or human health. Soil erosion without off-site effects has already been noted. In another example, farmers who operate tractors without sun protection thereby increase their risk of skin cancer. No externality is involved, and this environment-related health consequence of agriculture is not an appropriate target of government regulation. A reasonable case could be made for the government to distribute public health information, on the grounds that it would be relatively inexpensive, it would not be coercive, and there may be efficiencies to central coordination of such distribution. But if farmers are well informed on the subject, an appropriately constrained government should not try to influence the farmer's sun-protection decision.

Similar issues arise in consideration of farm workers' exposure to agricultural pesticides. Here, too, there may be information problems.[4] In the United States, such problems seem most likely where migrant farm workers do not speak English, and so information costs are especially high. (There may also be the problem of coercion of illegal aliens through exploiting their illegal status.) But the case here is no different, in principle, from that of the unprotected tractor driver. If the farm workers can be informed of the risks associated with exposure to farm pesticides, then there is no externality. Farm workers will weigh the monetary and nonmonetary benefits of farm

4. Antle and Pingali (1994) provide evidence from the Philippines that the costs of acquiring and assimilating information regarding pesticide use can be high and can lead to important health problems and productivity impairment. They argue that farmers with low stocks of human capital are likely to behave inefficiently in a changing environment and, in particular, with regard to their use of hazardous farm chemicals. Also see Antle (1994).

employment with the monetary and nonmonetary costs, and there are no third-party effects of pesticide application. Fraud is, of course, possible, but there are existing legal remedies for that problem. Although government-sponsored research and education on the risks of pesticides may be justified, with no externality to correct, neither more coercive efforts nor subsidies are justified.

The issues of the environmental effects of agriculture and appropriate public policy for dealing with them form a broad set. The focus of the present study is narrower: to analyze critically the often-heard claim that traditional farm programs exacerbate externality problems. In the pages to follow, I trace out the systematic environmental results from the programs and their recent modifications and focus on the results that likely generate externalities.

A Brief History of Commodity Programs

Current commodity programs had their origin in the Great Depression of the 1930s and the New Deal programs of the Roosevelt administration. Pasour (1990) discusses precursors in the earlier decades of the century, but the direct ancestors of the diverse commodity programs of today were those created in the Agricultural Adjustment Act (AAA) of 1933. In a time of disastrously low real commodity prices and widespread financial failure of farms, the AAA established the goals of supporting commodity prices to parity levels and increasing farm incomes.

The measures initiated by the AAA included production controls, price supports, and credit subsidies to farmers. While the stated and apparent goal of such policies was to alleviate the problem of low farm incomes, conservation goals became linked with farm programs early on. Bruce Gardner (1993) notes that the Supreme Court ruled the first attempts at supply control unconstitutional, which led to their replacement with acreage controls justified on grounds of soil conservation. Subsequent farm legislation has justified acreage controls on both supply control and conservation grounds. Still, the soil conservation aspects of agricultural policy before the 1970s are probably best viewed as public relations and not a motive force. It was the interests of commercial agriculture that were represented in the political negotiations drawing up agricultural policy.

Beginning in the mid-1970s, other interests, mainly consumer and environmental, became increasingly attentive to agricultural policy. By the time of the 1985 farm bill, such groups were well represented in Washington, and the 1985 Food Security Act contained environmental provisions of some consequence. Among these are, most notably, the Conservation Reserve Program and the conservation compliance provision, both discussed below.

The 1990 Food, Agriculture, Conservation and Trade Act continued the trend of increased involvement by environmental lobbying groups in the forming of agricultural policy. Delworth Gardner (1994) notes as significant that the title of the 1990 act contains the word *conservation* for the first time in the history of federal agricultural legislation, despite the numerous provisions of previous acts justified as conservation measures. Bruce Gardner (1993) documents the trend by listing the increasing frequency of reference to conservation and environmental goals in the titles of farm legislation since 1977.

2
Commodity Programs and Their Environmental Effects

Commodity programs are readily categorized by the instruments they use to support farm income. Below, I group the programs according to whether they explicitly support farm prices through deficiency payments, control supply with marketing quotas, or control the supply of imports with quotas. These are the traditional ways that economists have categorized commodity programs, and such labeling makes sense. Commodity programs were expressly designed, and have evolved, to affect or defeat specific market results.

The environmental effects of commodity programs, however, are their unintended consequences. Although the production of tobacco may have important external effects, for example, those effects have to do with the technology of tobacco production and the terrain on which it is grown. We have no reason to think that tobacco evolved as a supply-controlled commodity for any reasons related to the environmental effects of its production. While it is helpful to think generically about the effects on production and input use from, say, marketing quota programs (and such issues are discussed in some detail below), whether the production process generates environmental externalities will not be related to the existence of quotas. That is, the environmental effects of farm production are geographic and crop specific. Commodity programs, in contrast, cut across terrain by affecting markets. In this context, however, Reichelderfer (1990) argues that, by happenstance or not, the program commodities are, in fact, damaging to the environment:

> The mix of commodities receiving price support happens to include crops that are among the most soil erosive and chemically dependent of all agricultural land uses. By contrast, no production activities among the least erosive with low fertilizer and pesticide requirements receive price support. (p. 204)

Reichelderfer lists the following among the crops that either are "most erosive" or that have high relative fertilizer or pesticide requirements: cotton, soybeans, corn, and grain sorghum. Those considered least erosive and either low or lowest in relative fertilizer and pesticide requirements are grassland, hay land, range, and pasture. She concludes that agricultural policy, *circa* the 1985 Food Security Act, subsidized the production of the environmentally worst farm products and encouraged increased use of harmful chemicals.

Miranowski, Hrubovcak, and Sutton (1991) argue similarly, and in general terms, that corn is both erosive and more dependent on fertilizers and pesticides than nonprogram crops. They also point out that corn and cotton receive higher nutrient and pesticide applications than the other major program crops, soybeans and wheat. They consider all four crops to be more erosive than nonprogram crops.

One way to assess the broad environmental effect of commodity programs is to assess their production impact. If environmental externalities are generated by agricultural production, then removal of production subsidies should reduce the externalities along with production. The scale effect of program subsidies on production is tempered, however, by the fact that the major commodity programs employ acreage set-asides. Participants in the programs must agree to withhold from production some of their acres. Without commodity programs, set-aside land might be farmed. (And, as we shall see below, program payments that are not tied to production do not provide production subsidies in the first place. This point is particularly relevant for current versions of the deficiency payments programs.)

At an aggregate level, Miranowski et al. estimate the production effects of eliminating commodity programs. Using a computable general equilibrium model developed by Boyd (1987), they conclude that program crop production would decline by 7 percent in the long run if production subsidies were removed. Livestock production, they estimate, would decline by 2 percent.

Beyond scale effects, the ultimate consequences of production subsidies depend on how they affect the demands for inputs. Miranowski et al. consider such ultimate effects by analyzing how eliminating production subsidies would translate into factor demands. They conclude, for example, that the predicted 7 percent decline in program crop production would result in an 8 percent decline in chemical use.

Results from computable general equilibrium models and, indeed, any results at this aggregate level depend on assumed parameters. In this instance, what is critical is the substitutability assumed among agricultural inputs in the production of particular crops and the substitutability assumed among crops in consumer demands. According to Miranowski et al.,

> Differences in assumptions regarding substitution possibilities lead to quite different paths of

input use and output....For example, assuming no substitution among land, capital, and other manufactured inputs, output in the agricultural sector will increase after policy reform. The increase in available land after the [Acreage Reduction Program] is eliminated causes the demand for all inputs to increase. The combination of increases in land and nonland inputs causes output to increase. (p. 283)

Miranowski et al. treat in some detail as well the geographic distribution of production affected by such subsidies.

Still at the aggregate level, the environmental effects of commodity programs can be expected to change over time with market conditions. Just as the market effects of a price support program differ when the price support is binding from when it is not, the environmental effects of a price support program will vary over time.

Generic Effects of Increasing Price

Commodity programs increase equilibrium prices. The price increases are achieved through different mechanisms in different programs, and the ultimate environmental effects of the price increases are tied to the particular mechanism. Here, however, abstract from the specifics, and ask the general question, Does the government, by raising price above its unsupported level, encourage the production of environmental externalities? An affirmative answer to this question lies behind much of the environmental concern over commodity programs.

A link between price and environmental externalities presupposes an output-linked externality in the first place. Assume that such an externality exists, and consider the external effect to be related to the use of chemicals. Externalities are generated through runoff or leaching of chemicals, polluting either surface water or ground-

11

water. An increase in the commodity's price can be seen to influence chemical use on both the intensive and the extensive margins of production.

Consider the supply of the commodity to come from acres of cultivated land that differ from one another in the fertility of their soil. Assume that chemicals are substitutes for the quality of an acre's soil, at least at the margin: that an increase in soil quality will decrease the marginal product of chemicals. In a competitive equilibrium, the owner of each producing acre determines the optimal per acre application of chemicals by setting the value of the marginal product of chemicals equal to its price. Because we assume that chemicals and soil quality are substitutes at the margin, the owner of an acre with slightly better soil will rationally apply less chemical than the owner of an acre with slightly worse soil.[1]

In a competitive equilibrium, there is an equilibrium soil quality that earns zero rents in the production of the commodity. All acres inferior to the zero-rent acre will not produce the commodity, and all superior acres will. The zero-rent soil quality defines the extensive margin of production.

Now consider the effects of a program-induced increase in output price. Assume that the prices of inputs, including chemicals, do not change. There will be two effects. First, the higher output price will lead to a lower zero-rent soil quality. There will be acres that earned negative rents under the lower-price equilibrium and so did not produce the commodity; because the new higher price allows positive-rent production on some of those acres, they will produce. The aggregate amount of chemicals used in the production of the crop increases because of this expansion along the extensive margin, and specific externalities may result.

Second, chemical use also increases for those acres

---

1. Note that the two inputs, chemicals and land quality, could be complements for nonmarginal changes in the quantities employed.

of high enough quality to be producing both before and after the price increase. The increase in output price increases the value of the marginal product of chemicals on the inframarginal acres, and so there is an increase in chemical use along each producing acre's intensive margin. Preexisting externalities are made worse by expansion along the intensive margin.

As Antle and Just (1991) demonstrate and emphasize, the environmental consequences of agricultural policy depend on the geographic joint distribution of (here) chemical input use and the environmental attributes of the land, such as erodibility.[2] In our example, knowing the increase in aggregate chemical use is not the same as knowing what the external effects of the price increase will be. Land heterogeneity is important, and external effects of the price increase are site specific.

What aspects of land heterogeneity are important? And can the supply response on the extensive and intensive margins be expected to generate externalities? Among other things, one must know where the newly cultivated acres came from. If, for example, the price-supported commodity is corn and the extensive expansion came at the expense of land allocated to soybeans, then the generally acknowledged higher erosivity of corn could lead to external effects. In other cases, the extensive increase in planting of program crops could reduce externalities. If the acres were previously uncultivated, the original question must again be asked, Are there runoff or other external problems associated with production on the newly cultivated acres?

The relative importance of the intensive and the extensive margins depends on the distribution of land quality. If the distribution of land quality is thin near equilibrium, then most of the effect will be from more intensive application of chemicals to previously producing acres.

---

2. See also Antle and Capalbo (1992) on the evaluation of the external costs of agricultural chemicals.

Price and Income Support Programs

Deficiency Payments and Nonrecourse Loans. The bulk of government payments to farmers are made under a system of nonrecourse loans and deficiency payments. Recipients of these payments are growers of the so-called major program crops: corn, other feed grains (sorghum, barley, and oats), wheat, cotton, and rice. Notably absent from this list are growers of soybeans who receive, usually nonbinding, price support through nonrecourse loans but not deficiency payments. Helmberger (1991) discusses the evolution of this form of subsidy from the acreage restrictions of the 1950s.

Price and income support programs are important to the discussion of the environmental effects of agricultural policy for two reasons. First, the major program crops dwarf those covered by other programs, in government payments, market value, and in likely environmental impact. A simple measure of the size of government intervention in crop markets is the sum of payments to growers. In 1991, payments by the Agricultural Stabilization and Conservation Service were concentrated on growers of feed grains and wheat. Of the total of $8.2 billion paid to producers by ASCS in 1991, fully 70.4 percent went to producers of the major program crops. (The $8.2 billion total includes payments to farmers under the Conservation Reserve Program, which accounted for 20.2 percent of the total.)

Further, as a measure of the potential environmental impact, consider the extent of plantings. In acreage, wheat and corn dominate crop plantings. In 1992, planted acreage was 72.3 million acres for wheat and 79.3 million acres for corn. Other feed grains (oats, barley, and sorghum) were planted on 29 million acres, cotton on 13.3 million acres, and rice on 3.2 million acres.

The second reason to emphasize the major program

(or deficiency payment) crops is that current variants of deficiency payment schemes employ acreage diversion in the form of the Acreage Reduction Program (ARP) and other, more recent provisions. To the extent that environmental externalities of farm production are associated with the number of acres farmed (the extensive margin), then program effects on acreage have environmental consequences. Further, some variants of direct payment schemes, it has been argued, affect the intensity of production on whatever number of acres are farmed.

The deficiency payment crops are interesting here for yet another reason. Changes in the programs from the 1990 farm act, in particular "flex acre" provisions, have arguably lessened the environmental impact of deficiency payments.

How Direct Payments Are Determined. A generic model of a nonrecourse loan program with deficiency payments is as follows. The government sets a support price (equivalently, a loan rate), P_s, which is a price floor guaranteed to growers of the crop. If the market price should fall below P_s, then the government agrees to buy the production from program participants at P_s. What the government does with stocks purchased in this way is another issue and one with market, but not environmental, consequences. In modern versions of such programs, P_s is guaranteed on all production by program participants through the mechanism of nonrecourse loans. Farmers may borrow P_s per bushel that they "put under loan" after harvest. Later in the crop year, they can choose either to redeem their loan by paying back the money they borrowed including accrued interest or to forfeit the bushels they put up as collateral and fully discharge their debt to the government. They will exercise the second option when the market price has fallen below the loan rate plus accrued interest. (Another option exists under the marketing loan program; it will be discussed shortly.)

The deficiency payment to farmers is a transaction separate from the nonrecourse loan. It can be represented as:

$$\text{Payments} = [P_T - max(P_M, P_S)] \cdot A_E \cdot y_P, \qquad (2\text{--}1)$$

where P_T is a target price, P_M is the market price, A_E is the (eligible) acreage to which the deficiency payment is applied, and y_P represents (program) yield. The production and acreage effects of deficiency payment schemes vary with the rules that determine A_E and y_P. Both are important policy parameters with implications for external effects. Consider, first, y_P.

Program Yield. If acreage eligible for payments is somehow fixed, as it currently is, and if yield in the equation above is measured as the current year's actual yield on the farm in question,[3] then the payment scheme creates yield-increasing incentives. On fixed acreage, such incentives will increase the use of nonland inputs per acre, primarily chemicals—fertilizers and pesticides. If chemicals leave the farm site through direct runoff, percolation through the soil, or transport on eroded soil particles, then the yield increase can have external effects.

The size of the incentive to increase yield can be measured by the difference between the target price and what would be the market price absent the program. The marginal output price that determines the value of the marginal product of inputs is the target price, usually substantially above the market price. For example, the wheat target price has been $4 per bushel for several years,

---

3. An issue of terminology arises here. Some authors, Helmberger (1991, p. 204) among them, define direct payment programs to be those that calculate program payments according to the formula above using current actual yields. Others, such as Sumner (1990), draw no such distinction and refer to recent programs, which use historically determined yields, as both direct payment and deficiency payment programs (in contrast with programs that benefit farmers indirectly by increasing market prices).

while season-average wheat prices have ranged between $3 and $4. For corn, the target price is now and for several years has been $2.75 per bushel. The marketing year average price for corn has in these years been as high as $2.50. The 1994 crop price is forecast to be lower than $2 and, in certain areas, below the loan rate of $1.89.

The yield-increasing incentive comes from the direct link between production (yield) and the payments described in equation (2–1). If, however, current yield does not affect payments, then there is no incentive provided by the deficiency payments to increase yield. This has been the case since an important administrative change in 1986. Program yield at that time was frozen either at 90 percent of 1985 yield for the specific farm or at a historical county average yield. The rule change decreed that no variation in current yield was to affect program payments. Since then, payments have been determined by market prices, policy parameters (target prices), historical yields, and acreage base. None of these is influenced by the current year's production, and so there is no incentive provided by the deficiency payment to increase yield.

Reichelderfer argues that this change was significant. She suggests that "observed declines in total use and per acre application of agricultural chemicals since 1985 may be attributable, in part, to the 1986 freeze in base yields" (1990, p. 206). Delworth Gardner (1994), writing several years later, concurs: "The fertilizer data...are not inconsistent with the hypothesis that restrictions on program yields, and perhaps other factors...have been significant in stabilizing fertilizer use on American farms" (p. 28). This conclusion is supported by empirical evidence presented by Carlson, Gargiulo, and Lin (1994) and discussed below.

An intermediate case between the current policy of frozen program yields and one where current yields determine deficiency payments is one where farm yields are recomputed periodically. Recalculation might logically be done since technological change, in fact, increases yields over time. Before 1986, deficiency payment schemes periodically updated a farm's program yield to reflect such changes in technology and farming practice. The effect, at that time, of restricting acres through base restrictions was to induce farmers to increase current yields to increase future program payments. Again, because the environmental externalities of production can be linked to chemical use, the updating of base yields exacerbated the environmental effects of program crop production.

Base Acreage and Diversion. Return to the equation defining program payments to consider the other key policy variable, eligible acreage. The variable A_E could refer to actual planted acreage and, in fact, did in direct payment programs of earlier decades. Currently, the acreage used in determining deficiency payments is affected by several program provisions. Continuing the generic deficiency payments example, decompose acreage in the previous equation as:

$$A_E = A_b \cdot (1 - arp), \qquad (2\text{--}2)$$

where A_b is base acreage and *arp* (acreage reduction program) is the proportion of base acreage required to be diverted from crop production for participation in the program.

Base acreage is currently determined, for each of the major program crops, as a moving average of acreage planted to the crop. A five-year average, for example, is used for corn and a three-year average for cotton. Therefore, current deficiency payments are not linked to current acreage choice.

The term (1 - *arp*) refers to the Acreage Reduction Program, *arp* being the proportion of base acreage that the farmer must idle and plant in a cover crop to receive program payments. The ARP percentage can be changed administratively and is linked by formula to current stocks of the commodity. When stocks become large, the ARP percentage rises to restrict the next year's production. In some years and for some crops, the percentage is zero. For 1995 crops, *arp* will likely be zero for wheat, rice, and feed grains other than corn. The *arp* for corn and cotton will likely be 7.5 percent of base acreage.

For the participating farmer, the term $A_b(1-arp)$ imposes a maximum acreage to be planted to the program crop. The farmer may plant less but, with an exception to be discussed, does not receive deficiency payments on acreage he does not plant.

Despite the fact that the environmental effects of agricultural production are variable and site specific, it is tempting to generalize and to equate high per acre yields with environmental externalities. Much discussion of the environmental effects of farm programs revolves around whether the programs affect yields. Even as a rough approximation, however, it should be noted that not all program-induced increases in yields are correlated with chemical use. Under land diversion programs, farmers can be expected to divert land with the lowest opportunity cost. If soil quality varies across acres on a farm, then the least productive acres will be retired first. Accordingly, even with yields measured at the acre level held constant, yields per farm will rise with the number of acres diverted and with no environmental consequence.

The claim that farmers pay attention to land quality in their diversion decisions is not hard to believe. Whether or not higher diversion levels actually lead to higher farm yields is an empirical question, however. If it were the case that lower-yielding fields were also lower cost to cultivate, then one might not find a relationship between diversion rates and farm yields. Babcock, Foster, and Hoag (1993) provide farm and field-level evidence from North

Carolina that yields do, in fact, respond to diversion.

Flex Acres and the Determination of Base. The discussion to this point describes the deficiency payment schemes in the late 1980s. In the 1990 Omnibus Budget Reconciliation Act, the calculation of eligible acreage was further complicated by the introduction of "flex acres." The change was introduced primarily to lower the budget costs of deficiency payment programs. Secondarily, and of most interest here, it addressed the perverse environmental incentives due to base acreage calculations.

While the much earlier unlinking of eligible acreage from actual planted acreage was useful in controlling program costs, it unintentionally encouraged farmers to build base. Because deficiency payments are proportional to acreage base, base is a desirable commodity (see Duffy et al., 1994, who calculate its value). Because base is calculated as a moving average of recent plantings to the program crop, one strategy for expanding one's base is *not* to participate in the program for a year or more and, while not participating, to plant the program crop on a wide scale. During the base-building year, the farmer does not receive deficiency payments but does influence future base calculations. Base building can be thought of as investing in durable but depreciable rights to participate in the program and receive future deficiency payments. If one chooses one's base-building year carefully, or is lucky, and the market price is high during that year, then the opportunity cost of nonparticipation will even be small.

Base building has obvious government budget implications, but it also has environmental implications to the extent that it represents a scale increase in production associated with environmental externalities. Further, and beyond the scale effects of building base, base provisions offer incentives to cultivate the program crop continuously and not to rotate.

20

The incentive to build base induces more acreage to come into the program crop's acreage base. Once so classified, the moving average base calculation provides continued incentives to plant the program crop without rotation. In most instances, rotating crops reduces the desired application of pesticides and, with nitrogen-fixing crops, reduces the desired application of fertilizers as well. Encouraging unrelieved monocropping can, therefore, increase the external effects of production.

Those perverse and budget-straining incentives were addressed by the 1990 "flex acre" provisions. The basic effect of the provisions was to require farmers to divert planting of base acreage away from the program crop. The diverted acreage was to be planted (instead of to a cover crop) to either an alternative marketable crop or to the program crop but without receiving deficiency payments. Broadly, the provisions did two things: they reduced the incentive to participate in the program, and they reduced the program penalty for rotating crops for those who did participate.

There are two specific flex acre provisions: "normal flex acres" and "optional flex acres." (These are also known as the "triple base provisions.") Normal flex acres are better thought of as "mandatory" flex acres. The 1990 farm act required that 15 percent of base acreage be put in the category of normal flex acres.

A participating farmer is free to plant either the program crop or an alternative crop on normal flex acres, but he will receive no deficiency payments for the acreage. Normal flex acres are unambiguously bad for farmers who plant their usual flex acres in the program crop: they reduce the farmers' deficiency payments. For farmers who choose to plant their normal flex acres in an alternative crop, the normal flex acre option could enhance the value of participating in the program.

Optional flex acres, though, are good from the

farmer's view. The 1990 farm act allows up to 10 percent of base acreage to be designated optional flex acres, on which the farmer may plant either the program crop or an alternative crop. Unlike normal (mandatory) flex acres, optional flex acres planted in the program crop receive deficiency payments.

The effect of both types of flex acres on deficiency payments can be seen by revising equation (2–2) to reflect the current calculation of eligible acreage:

$$A_E = A_b \cdot (1 - arp - nfa - ofa_o), \qquad (2\text{--}3)$$

where *nfa* is the proportion of normal (mandatory) flex acres, currently .15, and *ofa*$_o$ is the part of the optional flex acre proportion (a maximum of .10) that is planted to a crop other than the program crop.

The important effects of both flex acre provisions are the decreased incentives to participate in the program and the flexibility allowed within the program for crop rotation. As should be clear, the potency of the incentives and additional flexibility in altering crop choice can be known only case by case. Results from Duffy and Taylor (1994), however, illustrate some important cases.

Duffy and Taylor analyze the probable effects of increasing the normal flex acre proportion from .15 (its current value) to .35. They analyze the effects on two operations, an Illinois farm that participates in the corn program and a southern Alabama farm that participates in the cotton program. The crop alternative for the corn program is assumed to be soybeans. The crop alternative for the cotton farm is assumed to be wheat and soybeans double-cropped.

Duffy and Taylor's dynamic programming results imply different optimal responses for different market conditions, but the general tendency in their simulations is for the increase in normal flex acres to increase the planting of nonprogram crops and to increase rotation. They summarize their results:

For the Midwest farm, in some cases, the optimal decision resulting from [an increase in the normal flex acre proportion] would be to drop out of the farm program for corn and plant the entire farm in soybeans. In other cases, the Midwest farmer would remain in the program but would expand soybean acreage through increased flex acreage in soybeans. For the cotton farm, the change in normal flex acres most frequently induces a change from full-farm planting in nonprogram cotton (for base expansion) to a strategy of remaining in program limits for cotton with the remainder of the acreage planted in wheat-soybeans double-cropped. (p. 57)

They also note that lower levels of pesticide use are implied by the shifts from corn and cotton to soybean rotations and to soybean-wheat double-cropping. They emphasize, however, the problems in generalizing about the environmental effects of such shifts. They point out that the erosivity of soybean production is often greater than corn but the erosivity of double-cropped wheat and soybeans is usually less than cotton. Therefore, the increase in normal flex acres would likely decrease pesticide use on the Illinois cotton-soybean farm but, at the same time, would increase the rate of soil erosion and, presumably, the off-site transport of the chemicals used. On the Alabama cotton farm, the chemical-reducing effect would be enhanced by the switch to a less erosive double crop. For that operation, the increase in normal flex acres would provide environmental benefits.

Duffy and Taylor also estimate the costs imposed by an increase in the normal flex acre proportions. Under typical market conditions, the per acre reduction in value for the Illinois corn farm was in the range of $4–20. The per acre reduction in value for the Alabama cotton farm was much higher, ranging from $80 to $90.

One other innovation of the 1990 farm act was the further decoupling of deficiency payments from production through what is now known as the 50/85 program for cotton and rice. The program allows growers who plant at least 50 percent of their maximum payment acres in the program crop to receive deficiency payments as though they had planted 85 percent of their maximum payment acres. Before the 1993 budget act, the 50/85 program was the 50/92 program. Versions of the feed grain programs in the late 1980s also had 50/92 provisions.

Marketing Loans. The freezing of base yields has gone most of the way toward eliminating any field-level bias in input use from deficiency payment programs. Deficiency payments are largely decoupled from production decisions, and the payments are simply transfers. Having no effect on the production of crops, they can have no effect on the production of externalities.

One could take several exceptions to this claim. The first concerns the support price (or loan rate). In recent years, the support price has turned out not to be binding and so, *ex post*, should not have had an effect on production. *Ex ante*, however, by truncating the bottom part of the price distribution, the price support may have increased plantings and the application of inputs with external costs.

Further, price supports sometimes bind. At the time of this writing, the 1994 bumper crop of corn had depressed prices to the point where the price support may have a real effect on price. The nonrecourse loans are not decoupled in the way that deficiency payments are. They apply to all the production of program participants.

One possible effect that the programs could still have is through their increase in the equilibrium price brought about through acreage restrictions. (I assume here that the acreage restrictions' effects on supply dominate any other production subsidy effect, for example, base building as analyzed by Duffy and Taylor.) The effect on program participants from acreage restrictions is unambiguously to shift the supply curve of participants to the left. The effect on participants, therefore, is to decrease their quantities supplied. There are substantial numbers of nonparticipants, however, who face a higher price because of the program. Thus, the higher equilibrium price will have an acreage effect on nonparticipants that could spread production externalities to areas that would not otherwise produce.

Finally, and as discussed in the section on the generic effects of increasing price, an increase in the equilibrium price will increase the value of the marginal product of fertilizer and pesticides on each acre and increase their quantities employed. This is a rather different effect from the incentive to increase yields on allowed acreage under a direct payments program, under which the target price determines the size of the incentive. Under a decoupled program, such as the current deficiency payment programs, the market price determines the size of the incentive. Therefore, to know by how much the programs distort the incentives at the field level, one needs to know by how much the programs increase equilibrium price and not by how much the target price is higher than the equilibrium price without the program. In sum, the aggregate effect of current deficiency payment programs is to reduce production. The acres that remain in production, however, will use more chemicals because of the price-increasing effects of set-asides.

The discussion above ignores one recent innovation in the deficiency payments programs: the marketing loan provision. Marketing loan programs, created in the 1985 Food Security Act, are an anomalous step away from the decoupling trends represented by base acreage and frozen program yields. Their implementation has made them relevant only for rice and cotton. The marketing loan provision encourages farmers not to forfeit their nonrecourse loans and does so by decreasing the price at which farmers may repay their loans. Throughout the marketing year, repayment rates are established slightly below the prevailing market price. Therefore, even when market prices are below the support price, farmers will repay their loans. The purpose of the marketing loan rate option is to minimize the stocks left for the government to dispose of. The effect of the option is to leave the deficiency–loan payment scheme not entirely decoupled. In net, farmers are guaranteed not just the support price for their production but the difference between the market price and the repayment rate in addition.

This last effect suggests a possible reform of the deficiency payment programs for rice and cotton that would be environmentally sound and would reduce government spending as well: freeze yields on loan payments as well as on deficiency payments. A farmer would no longer be guaranteed the support price on all that he produces but, rather, would be guaranteed the support price on a quantity determined by the product of his allowed acreage and a historically determined yield. This proposal would affect payments only when the market price fell below its support level. An equivalent proposal with much the same effect would be to scrap the nonrecourse loan–support price provision altogether. In its place, and on payment-eligible production, the new plan would pay P_T-P_M (target price minus market price), whether P_M is above or below a special support level. Either proposal would serve to decouple further the program payments from production decisions.

Chemical Use under Current Feed Grain Programs. The conventional wisdom holds that the feed and food grain programs encourage the application of yield-increasing inputs and discourage nonchemical means of pest control, such as crop rotation. Several arguments support the conventional wisdom, and, as we have seen, not all are germane to the programs in the 1990s.

Two plausible arguments still imply that current deficiency payment programs affect chemical use. The first is that farmers, to protect base acreage, are discouraged from rotating crops. As discussed above, the normal and flex acre provisions of the 1990 farm act deal with this disincentive to some extent, but individual farmers may still find the base restrictions binding and the program may discourage rotation.

The second argument refers to the incentives facing farmers to maximize the profit from market sales of their program crops. The argument is that set-aside restrictions affect farmers' optimal input mixture per acre. The optimal input choice on a 500-acre field, it is claimed, is not optimal on a 400-acre field, and a farmer will try to compensate for being restricted to farming only 400 acres by trying to increase his yield.

The argument implicitly assumes that the allocation of land is fixed and that the farmer in the example will not plant his 100 idled acres to a nonprogram crop. In the example, if there are alternative agricultural uses for the 100 idled acres and the nonland inputs, then the farmer should grow corn, say, on the 400 allowed acres using unconstrained profit-maximizing input ratios and grow other crops on additional acres (possibly the same 100 that are idled, given flex provisions) using the profit-maximizing input ratios appropriate to those crops. The farmer, then, would have no incentive to increase yield on the acres planted to program crops.

In contrast, if the idling of land through a set-aside leaves other nonland quasi-fixed inputs slack, perhaps management and capital, then farmers may substitute these underemployed inputs for chemicals on the farmed acres. One would find that set-asides actually decrease chemical use. Carlson et al. (1994) argue just this point in explaining empirical results that challenge the conventional wisdom.

Carlson et al. study recent state and farm-level data on insecticide use and crop rotation in corn. Drawing, in part, on results from Gargiulo (1992), they report that: (1) crop rotation rates are high—in most states and recent years, about 60 percent of corn acreage is planted on land that did not grow corn the previous year; (2) feed grain participation is positively correlated with crop rotation both over years and over states; (3) insecticide use is lower on rotated acres; and (4) corn insecticide use declined in the late 1980s.

The first two conclusions are those that challenge the conventional wisdom about the effects of feed grain programs. Coupled with the third conclusion, they imply that farmers in the feed grain program have lower rates of insecticide use. Consistent with this conclusion is the fourth result. The empirical fact that corn insecticide use declined in the late 1980s is particularly important for understanding policy effects because it may be explained by the freezing of program yields in 1986. Recall the claims by Delworth Gardner and Reichelderfer discussed earlier: that the freezing of yields stabilized or reduced chemical use in general. Carlson et al., too, conjecture that the freezing of yields was the cause of the reduced insecticide use in corn.

The main reason that Carlson et al. advance for their second result is the substitution of underemployed physical and human capital for chemicals, where the reason for the underemployment is the set-aside requirement. They offer another possible explanation of the second result, consistent with the frozen-yield explanation, that has implications for measuring the effects of commodity program reform. They argue that farm program participation may be more likely for better managers and that better managers are more apt to substitute their managerial skills for intensive pesticide applications. (They do not suggest why feed grain programs are more likely to recruit better managers.) If this second argument is correct, then the substitution away from chemicals is merely correlated with program participation and not caused by it. It suggests that the better managers would be substituting their abilities for chemicals whether or not there was a feed grain program.

The study by Carlson and his colleagues is among a small number that examine empirically rotation practices, chemical use, and program participation at the farm level. Another recent effort is that by Ribaudo (1994). Analyzing 1991 and 1992 field-level data for the major program crops, he found statistically significant increases in nitrogen, herbicide, and insecticide use associated with program participation. While his results do not directly contradict those of Carlson et al., neither do they support their conclusions.

Supply Control Programs for Tobacco and Peanuts

Tobacco and peanuts are the only two U.S. crops that are directly supply controlled. Direct control here means mandatory restrictions on the total quantity marketed (in the case of tobacco) or domestically marketed (in the case of peanuts). Unlike the deficiency payment programs, participation in the tobacco and peanut programs is, indeed, mandatory. The tobacco program is the only program to impose criminal penalties for noncompliance with its provisions (Foster and Babcock 1993). While only tobacco and peanuts are regulated by supply controls in the United States, international examples of supply-controlled commodities are numerous, including tobacco in Australia and tobacco, dairy products, and poultry in Canada.

Although the tobacco and peanut programs are quite similar, there is an important difference. The tobacco program limits by transferable quota the total amount that an individual farmer may produce and sell. The peanut program limits by transferable quota a farmer's sales to the domestic market. Anyone, quota owner or not, can grow peanuts in an unlimited amount and sell them for export or for nonedible uses in the United States.

Consider first the tobacco industry and tobacco program. Burley and flue-cured tobacco are the two main tobacco types grown in the United States. Together they account for about 80 percent of the total. The principal burley state is Kentucky, and the principal flue-cured state is North Carolina. There are distinct but similar programs for the two types of tobacco. Each employs individual quotas to restrict production directly.

One unit of quota can be thought of as the right to produce one pound of quota per year and to sell it to the government at a price supported above the world level. While the tobacco quota is almost universally discussed in terms of pounds, ownership of quota actually entitles the holder to a share of an aggregate quota, which is adjusted annually. Quota can be sold but only within county lines. At various times, there have been restrictions on the lease and sale of quota. (See Rucker, Thurman, and Sumner 1995 for an analysis of transferability restrictions.)

The aggregate effect of the tobacco program, then, is to restrict the quantity grown and sold in the United States and to increase its price. (The world price is increased as a result.) A secondary effect comes through the program's fixing of the geographic distribution of production. Because tobacco quota cannot trade across county borders, tobacco is grown now in approximately the same counties that grew it in the 1930s and in approximately the same proportions.

Any environmental effect of the tobacco program must come through the effect on crop choice in the tobacco-growing region. To the extent that alternative crops are more or less erosive, or more or less chemical intensive, tobacco supply controls may have external environmental effects. In sum, a direct supply control program such as the tobacco program should prima facie be viewed as environmentally benign.

Previous versions of both the tobacco and the peanut programs, however, controlled supply indirectly, through acreage allotments. Supply control of this sort should not be viewed as environmentally benign because of the effects of acreage restrictions on the use of nonland inputs, particularly pesticides and fertilizers.

Up until 1965, tobacco growers were required to possess acreage allotments for all their tobacco grown. The total quantity of allotments represented a binding restriction on the amount of land that could be planted in tobacco. Because the allotments were attached to the farms that held them, their value was capitalized into land prices. Growers of tobacco, therefore, paid higher land rents as a result of the program. Higher land values induced tobacco farmers to intensify their land input by using greater quantities of chemicals per acre and by more quickly adopting high-yielding varieties.

In 1965, the tobacco program ceased to require acreage allotments and instituted the output quota scheme now in place. At the time, as one might expect, tobacco land rents dropped dramatically. At the same time, tobacco yields, which had been growing steadily over the previous decade, dropped and stopped growing.

Foster and Babcock (1990; 1993) provide strong empirical support for the claim that tobacco yields were related to land prices, which were, in turn, related to the change from acreage allotments to poundage quotas:

We can conclude that the rapid growth in [to-bacco] yields from 1955 to 1964 can be attrib-uted to increasing land prices, wage rates, and yield potentials of available technology. The abrupt decline in expected yields in 1965 was coincident with a 92 percent decline in land rental rates with the corresponding drop in grower output price of 12 percent. (1993, p. 261)

The important difference between the tobacco and the peanut programs is that the peanut quota restricts sales only onto the domestic edible market. (See Rucker and Thurman 1990 for a fuller discussion of the peanut program.) If one owns (or rents) quota and sells to the domestic edible market, one is guaranteed the domestic edible support price, currently about $675 per ton. If one produces for the export market, which one can do without quota, the price in recent years has been near $350.

For most of the peanut-producing region, the envi-ronmental effects of the current peanut program are more likely to be benign than those of the tobacco program. The reason is that while tobacco quota restricts the quan-tity of tobacco supplied and so affects the distribution of crops grown in quota-owning areas, the peanut program probably does little to restrict the quantity supplied of peanuts. If peanut producers grow their quota amount as well as additional peanuts for the export market, then the marginal price they face is the $350 world price. With-out the quota restriction, producers would still face the same marginal price and would produce the same amounts. The effect of a quota and support price for do-mestic sales is entirely inframarginal and results only in a transfer of economic rents from domestic consumers to quota owners. If the peanut program influences the world price, which is at least questionable (see Rucker and

Thurman), then elimination of the program could have price and production effects.

Borges and Thurman (1994) argue that the peanut program is, indeed, inframarginal in its effects for North Carolina. From their analysis of county-level production and quota data, they conclude that the North Carolina peanut-producing counties regularly produce well in excess of their quota and that variations in the world price are far more important in determining variations in quantity supplied than are variations in the quota support price. Their results likely hold more strongly for the largest peanut-producing state, Georgia.

For some regions of the country, however, the quota support price is not inframarginal. In Texas and Oklahoma, there are counties where typically only the quota amount is grown and sometimes not even that. As one should expect, the rental rates for peanut quota in the area are low. In those areas, crop choice is affected by the peanut program in the same way that crop choice is affected everywhere by the tobacco program. Still, there is no obvious environmental externality generated by the production of peanuts instead of a substitute crop.

The Sugar Program

The sugar program limits the quantity of sugar imported into the United States, thereby raising the domestic price. The detailed policy is determined, first, by Congress, which sets the sugar support price in farm bill legislation. The support price typically exceeds the world price. The executive branch then creates import quotas so that the expected domestic equilibrium price reaches the support price. Import quotas are allocated annually to specific producing countries. In recent years, the domestic price of sugar has been about twice the world price.

The allocation of quotas to importing countries has

attracted the attention of economists over the years. (See, among others, Johnson 1974, Lopez 1989, and Leu, Schmitz, and Knutson 1987, who analyze the welfare effects and political economy of the U.S. sugar program.) Broadly, the quotas have increased the U.S. domestic price of sugar, reduced its consumption, and, important to the current discussion, increased its domestic production. Sugar is produced domestically from two sources, sugar beets and sugar cane. In recent years, about 60 percent of domestic production has come from sugar cane (USDA 1993).

The most publicized environmental effects of sugar production are associated with cane farming, especially near the Florida Everglades. In the United States, one-half of cane acreage is found in Florida. The remainder is split largely between Louisiana and Hawaii, with a small acreage in Texas. The environmental problems of cane production are primarily the large quantities of water used, often diverted from wetlands, and the nutrient loads added to water as it leaves sugar cane fields. Hahn (1992) argues that water management is the more critical issue of the two affecting the Everglades. The environmental problems of nearby Lake Okeechobee, also connected with sugar cane farming, derive from phosphorous levels that harm native plants by encouraging the growth of exotic species. Its artificial sources are several; fertilizer runoff from farms and effluent from sugar mills are the most important. Phosphorous is found naturally in soil and rainwater as well (see Boggess, Flaig, and Fonyo 1993). Of somewhat less concern is the air pollution from postharvest burning of cane.

The domestic environmental effects of the sugar program are attributable to the fact that more sugar cane and beets are grown because of the sugar price supports. It should be emphasized that this is purely a national accounting. Globally, the effect of raising the U.S. sugar price is to reduce consumption by U.S. consumers and so to reduce equilibrium global production of sugar. Without the sugar program, less sugar cane would be grown in the United States and more would be grown in, say, Mexico and the Caribbean. There are well-documented environmental problems with sugar cane production in those areas. See, for example, Arteaga (1993) and Little (1993).

How large is the effect of the U.S. sugar program on sugar cane acreage? Gemmill (1976) provides somewhat dated estimates of U.S. supply elasticities. Gemmill (1977) reports the cane sugar supply elasticity, averaged across U.S. supply regions, to be 1.57. A rough estimate of the increase in cane acreage can be obtained by applying this elasticity to the proportionate difference between the world price of sugar and the higher domestic price. In recent years, the price of sugar in Caribbean ports has been near 10¢ per pound, while the New York price has been above 20¢. If the sugar program were to disappear and the U.S. price were to fall to the world price, assuming that the change in U.S. consumption would not change the world price, the 50 percent price decline would result in a $1.57 \times (-50 \text{ percent}) = -78.5$ percent change in U.S. cane sugar production. If acreage declined in proportion with output, then the 450,000 acres in Florida planted in sugar cane would decline to under 100,000 acres.

The preceding calculation is obviously imprecise. It would be difficult to refine the calculation further, however, because the U.S. price has been supported by policy above current world levels for many years. To predict the effect of a 50 percent decline in price would extrapolate far outside any historical time series. Nevertheless, one can hardly doubt that the effect on U.S. production would be profound and that cane acreage, in Florida and elsewhere, would be greatly reduced. Along with acreage would be reduced the phosphorous runoff and other environmental problems of cane production.

There are, of course, policy options for dealing with environmental externalities from cane farming that have nothing to do with the sugar program. The usual command-and-control approach to environmental problems was typified by a plan drawn up for the Everglades in 1992 by the South Florida Water Management District. The plan called for specific regulations on farming practices as well as the conversion of large areas of farmland (about 56 square miles) to artificial wetlands that could emulate natural wetlands in their regulation of rainwater surges. This plan has since been modified in a 1993 agreement, brokered by the Department of Interior, among sugar growers, the management district, and the National Parks system (see *Sugar y Azucar,* August 1993).

Hahn suggests that tradable emission permits are an attractive alternative way to deal with phosphorous problems. The plan he proposes is similar to other tradable emission permit schemes. A target level of phosphorous emission into the watershed would be established, and that number of tons of credits would somehow be distributed to current businesses in the area. Monitoring stations would be set up at each potential emitter's site to enforce the limit on phosphorous emission.

Because the permits are tradable, a market in permits should develop to provide both the information and the incentives to trade and control and thereby to minimize the total cost of the phosphorous reduction. Firms, perhaps farms, with low costs of phosphorous control would find it profitable to sell, or at least not buy, permits. Other firms, with higher costs of phosphorous control, would be willing to purchase the permits to avoid having to engage in expensive control. Some elements of Hahn's plan have been incorporated into the most recent agreement.

If a tradable emission permit system were put into place in the Everglades, the market for permits would be affected by the sugar program and by any reforms in it. Indeed, there will be a policy interaction between the sugar import quota system and any independent effort to deal with the environmental problems of sugar cane farming. Consider the interaction between Hahn's tradable permit plan and the price of sugar.

If the sugar program were eliminated (or, less drastically, if import quotas were loosened), the derived demand for the assimilative capacity of the Everglades would be reduced. The demand for phosphorous permits as well as their rental rates and sales prices would decline. Such a reaction would be desirable from the viewpoint of economic efficiency, and the signals transmitted as a result of the permit price decline would provide socially useful information and incentives. The price decline, however, would also create a capital loss for the owners of permits. Permit owners would therefore be another vested interest and likely opposed to any moderation in the sugar program's import quotas.

Who would buy permits is hard to forecast. They would not necessarily be the users of the permits, the high-cost pollution reducers. They would be those who invest in buying the permits either for annual use or for leasing. If owners were also the annual users of the permits, they might be cane producers and processors, dairy farmers, or any other generator of regulated effluent. To the extent that transactions for permits are sales rather than annual leases, then the owners of permits would be nearly indifferent to the price of the asset. They would be both lessors and lessees of an asset, and changes in its price would have roughly equal costs and benefits.

Another instance of the inevitable but unforeseeable interaction of policy is the effect of extensive canal building. Much of the harm done to the Everglades is the result of drainage and transportation canals dug over several decades by the Army Corps of Engineers and funded by the federal government. Sugar cane production would obviously have a more benign environmental effect, and the sugar program could wreak less environmental damage, if the canals had not been built.

Dairy Policy

Dairy policy is complicated. It combines three approaches to farm income support: import restrictions, price supports through government purchases, and government-sanctioned and coordinated price discrimination between different end-use markets for milk. Dairying itself is one of the more environmentally costly agricultural activities. The combination of federal, and to some extent state, dairy policies has increased the scale of dairying operations over what they would have been without government intervention and has relocated dairy production. The scale and distributional effects of dairy policy have corresponding effects on aggregate externalities and their location.

The main environmental externality from dairy production is the same as that from other livestock operations: the discharge of animal waste into waterways or onto land. Runoff from dairy operations flows from pastures and, in more concentrated form, from barns. One problem that results from such discharge is the overloading of natural waterways with nitrogen and phosphorous compounds, collectively termed nutrients. Excess nutrient loads encourage algae growth, reduce dissolved oxygen, and degrade conditions for fish and other species. Another problem in some areas is the percolation of dissolved minerals into groundwater, contributing to the salinity of water supplies. Moffitt, Zilberman, and Just (1978) discuss the percolation problem in the Santa Ana river basin near Los Angeles.

The specific problems caused by runoff vary broadly by the concentration of dairying in the area, the assimilative capacity of the waterway, and the uses made of the waterway. One particularly well documented instance of the environmental problems of dairying is that surrounding Lake Okeechobee in south Florida. In the river basins draining into Okeechobee, production subsidies from both the sugar program and the dairy program combine to create external costs.

Boggess, Flaig, and Fonyo discuss the history of environmental problems and policy affecting Lake Okeechobee. They cite studies from the 1970s concluding that eutrophication of the lake was an important threat, that the primary enrichment problem in the lake was phosphorous, and that the primary sources of phosphorous were high-density dairy pastures and faulty dairy waste control systems. More recent studies cited by Boggess et al. report that phosphorous loading of the lake has increased over the past two decades and that agriculture is now the primary source of phosphorous entering the Lake Okeechobee watershed. Broken down by production activity, the major specific phosphorous sources are: improved dairy and beef cattle pastures (45.8 percent), sugar mills (15.2 percent), dairy barns (14.2 percent), and sugar cane fields (13.5 percent).

U.S. dairy policy will be described only briefly here. A fuller discussion can be found in Helmberger (1991). Two separate policies (plus import limits for cheese) constitute the heart of the dairy program. The first is a price floor on milk manufactured products: primarily butter, cheese, and nonfat dry milk. The price of manufactured products is supported by government purchases at announced support prices, implying that the federal government accumulates stocks. The federal government disposes of its acquisitions through donations to school lunch programs, distributions to the needy, and subsidized sales and donations to foreign countries. Import restrictions (authorized under section 22 of the U.S. Agricultural Act of 1993) protect the U.S. market for manufactured products from lower-price imports.

Much of the political history of the dairy program has been driven by periodic accumulations of government stocks at rates greater than the donation programs could dispose of. The price support program alone can be expected to lead to more milk production than would exist without the supports. Periodic attempts to reduce production offset this tendency. Recently, the milk diversion program (1984–1985) paid dairy farmers to reduce production from base levels, and the dairy termination program (1986–1987) paid dairy farmers to slaughter their herds and stop dairying for five years. Both programs were temporary and had temporary effects (see Baussell, Belsley, and Smith 1992).

The second major piece of dairy regulation is the system of federal milk marketing orders pertaining to sales of fluid milk.[4] While individual marketing orders cover limited areas, virtually all fluid milk is covered by one of the approximately fifty federal marketing orders or dozen state orders. The primary effect of the marketing orders is to discriminate by price between the two sources of demand for fluid milk: milk for consumption in fluid form and milk for use in manufactured products. Helmberger (1991) argues that, within each milk market and marketing order, the demand for milk for manufactured products is highly elastic and the demand for fluid milk is highly inelastic. The elastic demand for milk for manufactured products is due to the relative storability of manufactured products and the ease of transporting manufactured products across marketing regions. The inelastic demand for fluid milk is due, in part, to the perishability of fresh milk and its high transport costs.

4. A marketing order is a government sanctioned association of producers that collects and strategically markets the product of its members.

Given the differences in elasticity for the two derived demands for milk, a marketing order can increase total revenues to the member producers by restricting sales to the fluid market and raising its price such that the marginal revenue from fluid sales equals the marginal revenue from sales for manufactured uses. Assuming that the demand for milk for manufactured uses is perfectly elastic, a price-discriminating cartel could increase its profits by restricting sales to fluid handlers but not restricting the total sales to the two markets below what they would be under competition. In such a case, there would be no inefficiency in the total level of production. Further, there would be no reason to indict the marketing order for encouraging the generation of externalities.

The milk marketing orders, however, also employ blend pricing. The marketing order sells its fluid milk at a high price and its milk for manufactured uses at a low price. But the price per pound of milk that it pays its producing members is the marketing order's average revenue: a quantity-weighted blend of the two prices for which it sells. This weighting implies that the marginal incentive price that an order pays its members is higher than the marginal price at which the marketing order itself sells. That differential implies an inefficiency in the level of production by the order. Therefore, the marketing orders promote dairy production beyond that which would be expected from the price support of manufactured products alone and increase aggregate dairy runoff and its associated problems.

LaFrance and de Gorter (1985) measure from an aggregate econometric model of the U.S. dairy industry the effects of the dairy program. They do not address the issue of environmental externalities from dairy production but, usefully for our purposes, simulate the levels of dairy production that would have obtained without government intervention in the dairy market. Tables 2 and 3 in their article compare the historical sizes of the U.S. dairy herd with those predicted from the counter-factual simulation. They list herd sizes from 1965 through 1980. For the most recent years, during the late 1970s, they conclude that eliminating the dairy program would reduce herd sizes by 7 to 10 percent.

Finally, several authors (see West and Brandow 1964, and Ruane and Hallberg 1986) have argued that the dairy program has significant spatial effects. Without the program, they argue, milk production would shift away from certain regions, particularly the South and Northeast, and toward others, especially the upper Midwest and California.

Other Agricultural Policies

Other agricultural policies having environmental consequences, but not discussed here in any depth, include: marketing orders for fruits and vegetables, crop insurance and disaster relief programs (see Goodwin and Smith, *The Economics of Crop Insurance and Disaster Aid*, in this series of monographs) and federal land grazing policy.

It has been argued (see Reichelderfer) that fruit marketing orders encourage the overapplication of pesticides through imposed grading standards. If the pesticide application to fruit orchards results in external costs, then, by the usual logic, consumers of the fruit do not pay the appropriate price for cosmetically appealing fruit. If, however, the overapplication claim refers to consumer ignorance of the risk of pesticide residue on the fruit that they consume, that is another matter. Such an externality, if it is useful to call it such, is not driven by high contracting costs between the affected parties (fruit producers and fruit consumers) but rather by a lack of information. Noncoercive remedies, such as public education programs, could address the problem.

The issue for analyzing marketing orders is, if there is a production externality, whether the grading standards of the marketing order are more stringent than those that would arise simply from consumer valuation of blemish-free fruit.

3

Promotion of Environmentally Friendly Production

The Conservation Reserve Program and Related Programs

The Conservation Reserve Program is the most significant of recent attempts to integrate environmental concerns into agricultural policy.

Annual CRP payments to farmers to withhold cropland from production are now approximately $1.8 billion (fiscal year 1994), which represents almost one-quarter of total farm program payments from the Agricultural Stabilization and Conservation Service. Two related, but decidedly more minor, programs are the Wetland Reserve Program and the Water Bank. Under the Wetland Reserve Program, long-term easements are purchased from owners of wetland areas that preclude agricultural production. In exchange for annual payments, participants agree to restore and protect wetlands that they own. Payments under the Wetland Reserve in 1994 were $67 million. The Water Bank, similar to the CRP, contracts with farmers for ten years at a time to preserve wetland wildlife habitat. Payments under the program were $8 million in 1994.

The CRP in the 1985 Food Security Act. The CRP, created by the Food Security Act of 1985, revived the idea of the soil bank. The soil bank was created in the 1950s to deal with surpluses of price-supported commodities and, incidentally, with perceived problems of soil erosion.

There were two pieces to the original soil bank legislation. One created the acreage reserve, which annually paid producers of program crops (wheat, corn, rice, tobacco, and peanuts) to retire allotted acreage. The other created the conservation reserve. Under the conservation reserve, farmers signed contracts, from three to thirteen years in length, that called for annual payments from the government for acres that were not used to produce crops. The contracts further called for one-time payments to farmers who planted their retired acreage in grass, trees, or soil-conserving crops. While payments under the conservation reserve continued into the 1960s, no new contracts were signed after 1960.

The recent Conservation Reserve Program is similar to its previous incarnation under the soil bank, but with some differences. Most important is the way that contractual payments to farmers are determined. Because the process is closely related to the conservation and environmental benefits of the CRP, it is worth discussing in some detail.

The U.S. Department of Agriculture (USDA) was given substantial discretion over how to administer the CRP but was subject to the target levels of acreage enrollment specified in the 1985 Food Security Act. CRP administrators in the USDA devised a scheme to solicit bids from farmers to retire their land voluntarily from production for ten years. Enrolled land cannot be used for haying, grazing, or commercial crop production. Further, the land must be planted in grass or tree cover. In return, landowners receive annual rental payments and are reimbursed for one-half their conservation expenses.

Reichelderfer and Boggess (1988) discuss the key components of the USDA bidding scheme. First was an eligibility criterion. Land eligible for CRP contracts was that land eroding at rates more than three times a "tolerance" level, the rate at which the future productivity of the soil is not impaired. Farmers of eligible land submitted bids: offers of willingness to accept their stated amounts in return for idling acreage.

The second component of the implementation scheme was the size of the bidding pool. All bids less than a certain threshold were to be accepted for enrollment within a pool. Reichelderfer and Boggess explain the influence of political constraints on the determination of bid pools:

> The bid pools established for CRP bid solicitation and allocation in 1986 were defined by substate regions in order to assure a relatively equitable distribution of program benefits among congressional districts. (p. 3)

The third component was the setting of the maximum acceptable bid within each pool. It was determined in a way not to exceed prevailing rental rates in each region. Once the eligibility criterion and bidding pools were determined, the last component could be manipulated to determine aggregate program enrollment.

The setting of a maximum bid and the acceptance of all bids below the maximum distinguish the CRP bidding scheme from an auction. Under an auction, each successful bidder for enrollment would be paid his bid, not the poolwide maximum acceptable bid. Smith (1995) discusses these issues. He also analyzes the claim that enrollment offers far exceeded reasonable land rents in many parts of the country. His empirical analysis supports the claim. He concludes that "upper bound estimates of the cost of retiring 34 million acres [efficiently] [are] about $1 billion, a savings of approximately $600 million per year" (p. 20).

Note that the program differentiated only between the highly erodible land that was eligible to participate and land that was not. Once declaring certain acreage eligible, the program allowed the quasi-market process of bidding to enroll that acreage with the lowest opportunity cost, at least within a regional pool. Such a scheme minimizes the total costs of enrolling a given acreage but does not distinguish among tracts of land according to erodibility or, more important, to the off-site external effects of the tracts' erosion.

CRP Changes in 1990 Legislation. Most of the acreage now in the CRP was enrolled between the 1985 and the 1990 farm acts. Between 1986 and 1989, 34 million acres were enrolled. Since 1990, only 2.5 million acres have been enrolled. Osborn and Heimlich (1994) explain a difference between CRP enrollment under provisions of the 1985 act and enrollment under the 1990 act, a difference relevant to consideration of possible future versions of the CRP. They characterize the acres enrolled after 1990 as generating greater off-site (read *external*) benefits. This change resulted from the way bids for enrollment were accepted.

While CRP bids under the 1985 act were ranked only according to the dollar value of the farmer's bid, the ranking under the 1990 act was based on the ratio of an estimated environmental benefit per dollar spent by the government. The benefit was estimated by an index that gives weight to the surface and groundwater effects of crop production. This revision in bidding procedures led to a geographic shift in (the new and smaller) enrollment away from the Great Plains. Further, the 1990 act designated conservation priority areas that accounted for higher proportions of post-1990 enrollment acres. Among these are watersheds draining into the Chesapeake Bay, Long Island Sound, and the Great Lakes. One result was that the retirement of the newly enrolled acres primarily reduced water-caused soil erosion. The 1985–1990 enrollment primarily reduced wind-caused erosion.

Miranowski et al. (1991) characterized the CRP enrollments during 1985–1990 as geographically unrelated to problems of groundwater contamination by agricultural chemicals. For example, most of the Atlantic coastal plain, from Florida through Virginia, lies in an area of "potential groundwater contamination from agricultural chemicals" (see Nielsen and Lee 1987), while very little CRP enrollment during the 1985–1990 period came from the area. CRP enrollment was then, and remains, primarily from the Great Plains, from Texas up to Montana and the Dakotas. This area overlaps substantially the broad central belt of the United States where "concentrations of suspended sediment, nitrogen, and phosphorous can impair water uses" (Nielsen and Lee; see their figures 2 and 4).

Current Issues. The current CRP issue is the expiration of the ten-year contracts that were first signed in 1985. Osborn and Heimlich project the future expiration of CRP contracts. In 1995, contracts covering 2 million of the 36.4 million acres will expire. More than 22 million acres will come out of the CRP over the following two years.

A good deal of attention has been paid to the issue of what farmers will do with the acreage no longer under CRP contract. The Soil and Water Conservation Society queried more than 17,000 individuals in 1993 (5 percent of CRP contract holders). Two-thirds of the respondents said that they will return their CRP acres to crop production. Most of the remainder, it was reported, will be used for grazing or for the production of grass for hay.

Those who have praised CRP for its effects on soil erosion are, predictably, concerned about the effects of the expiration of contracts. Whatever the effects of CRP, they will expire along with the contracts unless the government signs up for another round of subsidy to nonproduction.

The forces behind a reauthorization of CRP are a coalition of environmental organizations and farmer groups. The National Farmers' Union, for example, has strongly supported an extension of CRP. A meeting of the governors of Western states in the summer of 1994 produced a statement that also strongly supported extending CRP. In partial response to this pressure, in early September 1994, Secretary of Agriculture Espy announced that CRP funding would be extended for one year beyond the ten-year limit.

A cogent criticism of CRP, at least its 1985–1990 version, is that retiring land is a rather blunt instrument to use to reduce erosion. If there are ways of farming highly erodible land that are not, in fact, highly erosive, then directly rewarding and subsidizing such practices could reduce erosion at a lower cost. Sinner (1990) makes just such an argument and claims that a targeted $200 million subsidy could have approximately the same effect on soil erosion as the $2 billion spent through the CRP for land retirement. In principle, targeted subsidies could better address particular externality problems in particular locales. In practice, it would be difficult to set general, nationwide guidelines for distributing subsidies in such a program.

A practical problem of a different sort is stressed by Gardner (1994). Highly critical of the CRP, he characterizes it as meeting only one of its stated goals well: that of providing income support for farmers. He argues, like Reichelderfer and Boggess (see the quotation above), that CRP payments are distributed broadly across congressional districts, while soil erosion problems are geographically concentrated. If implementable versions of CRP require broad geographic sharing of government payments, then narrow targeting of, say, eligibility criteria is not feasible.

Finally, one must ask if the goal of CRP, reducing soil erosion, is per se a good thing. The germane policy question is whether any particular instance of soil erosion constitutes an externality. If wind erosion, for example, blows topsoil off some exposed acres and relocates it to adjacent acres within a farm, there is no externality. The farmer who owns both the eroding and the soil-receiving acres bears all the costs and benefits of his farming. We should rely on him to undertake appropriate value-maximizing actions to prevent soil erosion at the eroding site.

On the nonexternal effects of soil erosion, Crosson (1991) provides some evidence on the desirability of not doing much more than is now being done. He estimates that the costs of soil erosion, due to lost future productivity, over the next 100 years will be between 1 and 2 percent of the costs of production. This estimate at least makes plausible the assertion that farmers are not irrationally ignoring the present-value implications of erosive cropping practices.

The problem of externality in soil erosion occurs when downwind or downstream deposition of soil particles has harmful effects. If they do, and if the upwind and downwind parties are prevented by transactions costs from contracting over erosion's effects, then a prima facie case can be made for public action. Osborn and Heimlich suggest that the external effects of soil erosion are associated primarily with water erosion and not with wind erosion. This makes particularly important their claim that the post-1990 CRP enrollment was successful in targeting acres subject to water erosion and, hence, external effects.

Conservation Compliance

The conservation compliance provision of the 1985 Food Security Act encourages farmers to draw up and carry out approved conservation plans by withholding farm program benefits if such a plan is not in place and carried out. The act required the establishment of a plan by 1990. It called for denial of benefits if the plan had not been implemented by December 31, 1994.

Conservation compliance specifically targeted lands that were identified as highly erodible, measured by an erodibility index. The erodibility index measures the erodibility of a soil in its uncultivated state relative to the amount of erosion consistent with undiminished production. An erodibility index value of 1 implies that, without conservation effort, the soil erodes at exactly the rate that would leave crop production unchanged. Higher values of the index imply a deterioration in the fertility of the soil. The definition of "highly erodible" under the 1985 act came to be soil with an erodibility index of 8 or greater. A 1982 inventory of cropland identified 118 million acres that were highly erodible in this sense.

Enforcement of the conservation compliance provision is carried out by field offices of the Soil Conservation Service.[1] To approve or disapprove conservation compliance plans, they use criteria that can include the financial burdens imposed by carrying out conservation activities on particular farms.

The incentives provided by conservation compliance and the Conservation Reserve Program are symmetric for acres deemed highly erodible. Conservation compliance constitutes a penalty for not controlling erosion on erod-

---

1. The Soil Conservation Service, following a USDA reorganization, now goes by the name of the National Resource Conservation Service. Throughout the discussion here, I use the older term, Soil Conservation Service or SCS, to refer to the service both before and after the name change.

ible land. The conservation reserve creates a positive incentive for redirecting land from eroding use to less eroding or noneroding use, primarily the growing of cover crops such as grasses.

Not only do the two programs aim for the same broad objective, reducing soil erosion, but the provisions of each influence the behavior of farmers with respect to the other. In fact, the conservation compliance provisions were suggested initially as a way to reduce the Treasury cost of the CRP. It was felt that owners of highly erodible land would face lower opportunity costs of enrolling their land in the CRP if their alternatives were to farm and receive commodity program payments subject to costly conservation compliance. The lower opportunity costs for highly erodible land should, then, reduce the CRP bids of owners of such land, making highly erodible land available to the CRP at a lower annual rental rate.

The effect of conservation compliance on CRP bids from highly erodible lands has not been verified, and, indeed, it is hard to imagine how it could be. Both CRP and conservation compliance were created in the 1985 act, and only their joint effects could be measured. Further, it seems unlikely that the conservation compliance provision affected CRP payments because of the administration of CRP as an offer, instead of an auction, system (see Smith 1995).

Now that CRP funding may well lapse and lands enrolled in the CRP may return to production, another interaction between CRP and conservation compliance arises. If CRP fades away over the next ten years, owners of CRP-enrolled land will face the decision of whether to return their land to production. Not all land in the CRP is highly erodible (approximately 27 million acres out of a total CRP enrollment of 36.5 million acres), but that which is will face the costs of conservation compliance if it comes back into production. The disincentive from conservation compliance may keep acres out of production even after CRP payments cease.

Has conservation compliance succeeded in reducing erosion from farmlands? That question is hard to answer for two reasons. The first is that the deadline for implementing conservation was December 31, 1994, only recently past at the time of this writing. The second is that there was no attempt to compile farm-level data on actual erosion before and after conservation plans were implemented. Nonetheless, administrators of the program in the Soil Conservation Service (SCS) have claimed great success.

In North Carolina, Cecil Settle, acting state conservationist for the SCS, reports in a June 1994 issue of the *Carolina Farmer*: "North Carolina farmers have done an excellent job of applying the needed practices....By targeting cropland with the highest erosion rates, the [conservation compliance] provision is making an important contribution toward improving our state's water quality." The article goes on to report the findings of an SCS report that concludes that erosion rates on the 1.5 million acres of highly erodible cropland in North Carolina have dropped by 60 percent since the 1985 enactment of conservation compliance.

An article in a June 1994 edition of the *Southeast Farm Press* replays the congratulations for Alabama. Reported there is an estimated decrease of 63 percent in erosion rates on 1.6 million highly erodible acres in Alabama. According to SCS Alabama State Conservationist Ernest Todd, 95 percent of the Alabama conservation plans are being carried out on schedule. Todd "commends the farmers of Alabama for the excellent progress they have made in implementing their conservation plans."

The state conservationist in Arkansas, Ronnie D. Murphy, similarly reports, "Overall, we feel that our Food Security Act conservation compliance efforts have been very successful since 96.3 percent of the tracts that were status reviewed were found to be 'actively applied'" (cited in Cook and Art 1993, p. 32).

Not everyone is convinced that conservation compliance has resulted in large environmental benefits. A sharp attack on the enforcement of conservation compliance by the SCS comes from Kenneth Cook and Andrew Art at the Center for Resource Economics. They view the measures of success reported by SCS administrators as measuring only lax enforcement. Cook and Art do not have independent verification of the extent to which farmers are abiding by the conservation compliance provision. They point out that only minuscule amounts of farm program payments have been denied under the conservation compliance provision and that this is prima facie evidence that local SCS officials are colluding with farmers to circumvent the law. They bolster their argument by citing a 1992 audit by the USDA Office of the Inspector General, which criticized the SCS field offices for their enforcement procedures. Cook and Art conclude:

> It is highly probable that in 1992, as in 1991, tens of thousands of farmers received hundreds of millions of dollars in farm program benefits for which they should not have been eligible because they were not complying with sodbuster, swampbuster, or conservation compliance provisions of federal law. (p. 1)

It is not clear what should be made of the enforcement issue. It is plausible that local conservation service officials would not adapt immediately or well to a role of enforcing conservation compliance. Further, monitoring farm-specific plans is costly to do and costly to oversee. Recent support for Cook and Art's criticism of SCS comes from a General Accounting Office study that concludes that cultural conflict between SCS's traditional role as a provider of technical assistance and its newer enforcement role "is believed to have led to an under-reporting of violations in order to avoid citing farmers for violations" (*Southeast Farm Press*, December 1994).

Beyond the specific issue of enforcement, there is a generic and cogent criticism of using the denial of farm program payments to enforce environmentally friendly production: the loss of program benefits may be costly at some times and not so at others. That criticism applies both to the conservation compliance provision and to the sodbuster and swampbuster provisions. In the case of deficiency payment programs, the incentive to conserve will be high when the market price is low and low when the market price is high. The environmental effects of such policies can be expected to be variable and highly uncertain.

Similarly, the disincentive from withholding program payments varies not only over time but also across crops. If commodity programs are used to achieve other than environmental ends, as they are, then the environmental payoff to measures such as conservation compliance will depend on market conditions that are only partially related to the costs and benefits of erosion control.

Swampbuster and Sodbuster Rules

The swampbuster provision of the 1985 Food Security Act denies practically all farm program benefits to those who farm land designated as a wetland. Likewise, the sodbuster provision denies benefits to farmers who convert highly erodible grasslands to cropland. Benefits denied to sod- and swampbusters include price and income supports, crop insurance, farm storage loans, disaster relief payments, and Farmers Home Administration loans. Both provisions took effect in December 1985.

Delworth Gardner (1994) points out that about 80 percent of U.S. farmers are beneficiaries of some farm program. He also points out that the sodbuster and swampbuster penalties stipulated in the 1985 Food Security Act were substantially reduced in the 1990 Food, Agriculture, Conservation, and Trade Act.

Interactions with Broad Environmental Programs

Provisions of farm acts are only part of the environmental regulation of agriculture and, at least until recently, the least important part. Major federal environmental legislation that regulates agricultural production includes the Federal Insecticide, Fungicide, and Rodenticide Act, the Clean Water Act, the Clean Air Act, the Endangered Species Act, and the Coastal Zone Management Act. Environmental regulations, having dealt with automobiles and so-called point sources of pollution for two decades, are increasingly focused on nonpoint sources, agriculture being the leading case. Each of these broad environmental measures interacts with the environmental provisions of farm law, and the political fates of the environmental and farm legislation are linked as well.

The fate of the Clean Water Act is particularly important. Senator Patrick Leahy of Vermont is quoted in a July 25, 1994, issue of *Roll Call* as saying, "I drafted the 1990 farm bill with the Clean Water Act in mind. It is my intention that the 1995 farm bill continue this effort."

The legislative forecast as of early 1994 was that the Clean Water Act would be reauthorized well before congressional debate on the farm bill. The Clean Water Act has since been stalled and will not be reconsidered until the new congressional session in 1995, but likely before the farm bill. Significantly, many view the farm bill and the Clean Water Act as regulatory substitutes in the production of agricultural environmental legislation. Some believe that the 1995 farm bill can address some of the same water quality issues as the Clean Water Act. The political pressure to address environmental problems through farm programs has therefore increased.

4
Proposed Environmentally Friendly Agricultural Programs

Those who advocate the marrying of current commodity programs to environmental objectives see the possibility of simultaneous progress on at least two social projects: supporting the income of farm operators and improving environmental quality.

Promises of Green Support Programs

The Campaign for Sustainable Agriculture, an umbrella group of over 200 organizations supporting environmental agricultural policy change, lists a number of objectives that it simultaneously seeks to meet. The campaign "is committed to a farm and food system that:

- supports stewardship of the land and its resources.
- combines economic viability with environmental soundness and social justice.
- promotes family farm and rural community economic opportunities.
- optimizes the use of on-farm and renewable resources.
- ensures a safe and abundant food supply produced under safe working conditions and with

fair pay for all workers and humane treatment of animals.
- provides consumers with adequate information to make informed choices.
- maximizes social, environmental, and economic benefits from limited public funds committed to food and agricultural programs." [Campaign for Sustainable Agriculture 1994]

One interpretation of the goals of the campaign is as the union of the goals of its constituent organizations. Every organization can point to one of the goals as its primary interest and can support the coalition as long as it does not actually oppose other goals on the list. An individual group may be primarily interested in, say, animal welfare but not particularly interested in increasing family farm income. The campaign might then be viewed simply as a collection of strange bedfellows who find cohabitation mutually beneficial.

The literature of the campaign taken at face value, however, suggests that the listed goals are consistent and that agricultural policy, if carefully fashioned, will promote small, wise, and profitable farms at the same time that it prevents environmental abuse. The realities of the environmental externalities generated by agriculture suggest otherwise.

Lynch and Smith (1994) compare the geographic distribution of the environmental effects of agriculture with the geographic distribution of farm program payments using county-level ASCS data. They use an environmental benefits index developed by USDA's Economic Research Service to measure the environmental impact of agriculture and weight the index by affected population. Assuming that marginal damage from agricultural externalities is correlated with total damage (as measured by the environmental benefits index), they conclude that a "green support program" that maximized environmental quality would be concentrated in the heavily populated Northeast and Chicago lake plain, the southern Piedmont, the Mississippi delta, and parts of southern California and south central Arizona. Conspicuously absent from this list are the major payment-receiving regions in the Great Plains. Lynch and Smith conclude:

> In some cases (e.g., south Central Arizona, California's Central Valley) there is an overlap between areas of concentration of farm program benefits and areas in which the composite index of environmental problems is very high. However, targeting green support program payments by the current distribution of commodity program payments would mean a sacrifice of improvement in environmental quality, as measured against the distribution that would garner highest expected environmental benefits. (p. 7)

To proponents of green support programs, the low spatial correlation between current program payments and agricultural externalities presents a formidable problem. If one views current commodity programs as effectively addressing the farm income support goals of the nation, then the current distribution of payments is geographically appropriate. If one also agrees that subsidies for environmentally friendly farming are needed mostly elsewhere, then it is hard to imagine green support programs that can meet both income and environmental objectives without breaking the federal budget. Subsidizing particular people, defined by socioeconomic and demographic characteristics, is different from subsidizing particular activities.

If one more cynically views current commodity programs as simply a political equilibrium (for elaboration see Bruce Gardner 1987), then a no less formidable problem arises. One may wish to redistribute farm subsidies to areas where the value of externalities is large and to subsidize certain production techniques in those areas, but that implies redistributing income away from current members of a politically powerful coalition. At the outset, then, one must doubt either the efficacy or the political feasibility of a green support program that attempts to address both income support and environmental externality problems.

Lessons learned from the decoupling debate are useful here. Many have advocated decoupling farm subsidies from production outcomes on economic efficiency grounds: that lump-sum subsidies transfer income more efficiently than subsidies that distort market signals. Recent and proposed agricultural policy reform represents movement in this direction. In particular, current deficiency payment and loan schemes improve on their predecessors by decoupling current payments from current production outcomes.

There is a parallel, and powerful, argument for decoupling farmer income support programs from programs addressing agricultural externalities. In this case, the goal of the environmental program should be to alter the incentives that farmers face so as to substitute for a missing market incentive. Stated this way, this is fine-tuning of the highest and most demanding order, and one should be skeptical of the ability of any program to provide such a finely tuned signal. (Skepticism is particularly appropriate when one considers the information and transactions costs that led to the problem of externality in the first place.) But regardless of one's optimism toward the ability of government to solve externality problems, the problem of policy design can only be made more difficult by coupling environmental goals with the goal of supporting certain farmers' incomes in certain regions.

Examples of Green Support Programs

Graduated Deficiency Payments. The idea of graduated deficiency payments is to increase target prices to farmers who do particular environmentally good things, like adopt whole-farm conservation plans. Part of the package might be to exempt such individuals from payment limitations as well.

The graduated deficiency payment proposal resembles the current conservation compliance provision (discussed above), which requires farms to file and implement conservation plans to qualify for farm program payments. While conservation compliance represents a stick, graduated deficiency payments represent a carrot. Both incentives are tied to participation in the commodity program, and so their effectiveness depends on how attractive participation in the program is. As discussed above, the appeal of participation depends on market prices and other factors that are only partly related to the marginal costs and benefits of environmental externality control.

The graduated payments scheme, as a carrot, does not suffer from the defect that it might discourage commodity program participation. If the environmentally related deficiency payments are true bonuses on top of ordinary payments, then they can only encourage the activity subsidized. Of course, if graduated deficiency payments were adopted as a quid pro quo for the elimination of ordinary deficiency payments, the costs of participation would be affected. Again, the program runs the risk of driving away those who would find the environmental measures expensive. Linking commodity program payments to environmentally friendly behavior provides no incentive to those outside the program.

Environmental Reserve. "Environmental reserve" has been used to describe various plans, few described in detail. One version of it would link set-aside levels, required for participation in deficiency payment programs, to the environmental effects of bringing land into production.

The proposal would require assigning to particular acres or fields an "environmental hazard score." That score, for example, could be the same erodibility index used in the definition of highly erodible lands under the conservation compliance provision. An acre with an index value of 1.0 could count as one erodible acre. An acre with an index value of 2.0 could count as two erodible acres, and so forth. The environmental reserve approach to set-aside might say that, in a particular year, for every erodible acre planted to a program crop, .20 of an actual acre would have to be set aside. Producing on one acre with an erodibility index of 2.0 would be allowed by setting aside .40 of any other acre in the producer's base. This approach would encourage planting by an individual farmer on the least erodible acres and the retiring of the most erodible acres. Further, the effect across farms would be to increase the costs of program participation to farmers of erosive soil.

The effect on a cross section of farmers highlights, again, one of the generic problems of linking environmental rewards with farm program payments. It is tempting to try to fine-tune environmental incentives to achieve the greatest environmental benefit at the least cost. The environmental reserve proposal refines the current acreage reduction program along these lines. By trying to discourage production on environmentally fragile lands, however, one may simply raise the costs of program participation to farmers on such lands and induce them not to participate. While one solution would be to make participation in farm programs mandatory, the green payment option then resembles more closely the command-and-control approach that advocates of green payments and others criticize.

Super Compliance Requirements. The super compliance proposal is to fortify the current conservation compliance requirements from the 1985 Food Security Act. Among commonly mentioned items that might be required to satisfy the conservation compliance criteria are the planting of shelter belts and filter strips and lowering the use of fertilizers and pesticides.

Green Payments. Certain environmental incentive schemes are naturally viewed as modifications of existing farm programs. Specific green payment proposals in this category include, for example, the graduated deficiency payment scheme discussed above. That proposal is presented as an add-on to current feed and food grain programs. The general category of green payments, however, refers to any positive incentive provided to farmers for undertaking production practices deemed environmentally friendly.

Some authors have noted that green payment programs would allow the United States to circumvent restrictions on price distortions set in place by the General Agreement on Tariffs and Trade (GATT). Currently, the GATT calculations of effective rates of protection by the United States do not require the dismantling of any commodity programs. Should such a restriction begin to bind, however, green payments might become attractive to those seeking to protect domestic farm producers.

Bushel-based Supply Management. The term *bushel-based supply management,* as used by some, refers to direct controls on farmers' marketable production. It also describes the current programs for tobacco and peanuts. Some argue that the environmental benefit from converting the feed and food grain programs to direct supply controls would be the removal of any incentive under existing deficiency payment programs to increase yield and to monocrop. Whether there is such an incentive is in dispute (see the discussion above on the effects of frozen yields and flex acre provisions).

It is argued above that direct supply controls should be expected to be environmentally benign, neither adding to nor subtracting from environmental externality problems. For the same reasons, unless quotas were established for all environmentally damaging crops, the case for bushel-based supply management on environmental grounds appears weak.

5
Conclusions

I conclude with two broad questions. First, do farm programs exacerbate environmental externalities and, if so, can they be altered to reduce their environmental harm? Second, should farm programs be used as tools with which to address environmental externalities?

Changes in Farm Policies

We have good reasons to believe that major crop farm programs in the past, through their effects on yield-increasing chemical inputs and through their discouragement of crop rotations, raised the external costs of agriculture. Most of the yield-increasing incentives, however, are gone from current versions of the programs. The supply control programs no longer rely on acreage allotments and already employ what proponents of green payments have dubbed bushel-based supply management. More important (because of the size of the feed grain and food grain sector), the deficiency payment programs are no longer direct payment programs. They no longer base payments on realized yield and no longer provide that incentive to apply yield-increasing chemicals. Further, through the recent flex provisions, they now allow some rotation of crops within a farmer's acreage base.

The reforms in the deficiency payment and supply control programs, we should note, were adopted primarily for budgetary reasons. The yield-increasing effects of both sets of programs were bad for the Treasury at the same time that they were bad for the environment. Just as the environmental effects were unintended consequences of agricultural policy, their partial alleviation was an unintended consequence of agricultural policy reform.

Not all is environmentally well with current farm programs. It is still true that a program that encourages domestic production of a commodity that generates negative environmental externalities can properly be blamed for making environmental problems worse. The dairy program and its production incentives are a case in point. The U.S. sugar program, which protects the domestic sugar industry but fails to protect the environmentally fragile lands on which sugar cane is grown, is another example. The standard aggregate welfare-maximizing argument for doing away with import restrictions is strengthened in the sugar case where the domestic protection causes environmental harm. There is no reason to think that the environmental effects of sugar cane production in other countries, however, are less costly to the citizens there than they are to citizens of the United States.

A successful environmental reform appears to be the post-1990 version of the Conservation Reserve Program. The CRP established in 1985 has been widely and justifiably criticized for buying little environmental bang for the buck. It appears, however, that the expenditures on land enrolled after the 1990 farm act bought more. Admittedly, the post-1990 version was much more modest than the 1985 version. (Only 2.5 million acres were enrolled after 1990 compared with 34 million acres before.) But the acres enrolled have, by design, been those responsible more for water erosion than for wind erosion, thus being more responsible for off-farm externalities, and have been located where agricultural runoff causes greater harm.

The Route to Environmental Reform

The examples cited of frozen yields, conversion of acreage controls to output controls, and flex acre provisions demonstrate that environmental reform of commodity programs is possible. Agricultural commodity programs can and have been made more environmentally friendly, and there is further room for improvement. But this conclusion does not imply an answer to the question whether farm programs should be used as tools to address environmental externalities.

There are several reasons for thinking that farm programs should not be so used. For one, there are no programs for the beef, pork, and poultry industries. All three are growing—pork and poultry rapidly—and all three produce concentrated animal waste, which causes locally important surface water, groundwater, and odor problems. Externalities generated by these industries cannot be addressed by farm programs unless we are willing to widen the ring of government subsidy to include them.

Another problem with building environmental incentives into farm programs is that the inherent time variation in farm program payments limits their value in correcting environmental externalities. The traditional rationale for farm programs has been to correct distributional problems created by the workings of markets. To the extent that that rationale continues to justify these programs, the specific subsidies they offer will be tied to market conditions. The rewards to farming in environmentally benign ways will thus necessarily be tied to market conditions. The environmental benefit will then be tied to conditions that may have something to do with the costs of environmental controls but little to do with their benefits.

Finally and, perhaps, most important from the view of those seeking genuine environmental improvement is an issue of truth in labeling. If farm programs are sold to the public on the grounds that they are buying environmental quality, the public is bound to be disappointed. As argued in chapter 4, making payments to the traditional coalitions supporting farm programs is a different task from making payments to promote environmentally friendly production or from penalizing environmentally unfriendly production. The attempt to make farm programs "green" can only disappoint citizens interested in improving environmental quality.

Sumner (1990), in a discussion of the distribution of program benefits across farm sizes and wealth, concludes that means other than commodity programs may achieve distributional objectives better than commodity programs themselves. The same can be said of environmental objectives. In a phrase that arises frequently in discussion of these issues, commodity programs are "blunt instruments" for dealing surgically with the adverse effects of farming on the environment.

References

Antle, John M. "Choice, Efficiency, and Food Safety Policy." Paper presented at the American Enterprise Institute conference, "Future Directions in Agricultural Policy," November 3–4, 1994, Washington, D.C.

Antle, John M., and Susan M. Capalbo. "Physical and Economic Model Integration for Measurement of the Environmental Impacts of Agricultural Chemical Use." *Northeast Journal of Agricultural and Resource Economics* 20(1992):68–81.

Antle, John M., and Richard E. Just. "Effects of Commodity Program Structure on Resource Use and the Environment." In *Commodity and Resource Policies in Agricultural Systems,* edited by R.E. Just and N. Bockstael. New York: Springer-Verlag, 1991.

Antle, John M., and Prabhu L. Pingali. "Pesticides, Productivity, and Farmer Health: A Philippine Case Study." *American Journal of Agricultural Economics* 76(1994):418–30.

Arteaga, V. "Environmental Impact of Sugar Cane Production in the Central Region of Venezuela." Proceedings from the technical program of the Inter-American Sugar Cane Seminar, 1993.

Babcock, Bruce A., William E. Foster, and Dana L. Hoag. "Land Quality and Diversion Decisions under U.S. Commodity Programs." *Review of Agricultural Economics* 15(1993):463–71.

Baussell, Charles W., David A. Belsley, and Scott L. Smith. "An Analysis of 1980s Dairy Programs and Some Policy Implications." *American Journal of Agricultural Economics* 74(1992):605–16.

Boggess, W.G., E.G. Flaig, and C.M. Fonyo. "Florida's Experience with Managing Nonpoint-Source Phosphorous Runoff into Lake Okeechobee." In *Theory, Modeling and Experience in the Management of Nonpoint-Source Pollution.* Boston: Kluwer Academic Publishers, 1993.

Borges, Robert B., and Walter N. Thurman. "Marketing Quotas and Random Yields: The Marginal Effects of Inframarginal Subsidies on Peanut Supply." *American Journal of Agricultural Economics* 76(1994):809–17.

Boyd, R. "An Economic Model of Direct and Indirect Effects of Tax Reform on Agriculture." USDA-ERS Technical Bulletin 1743, Washington, D.C., 1987.

The Campaign for Sustainable Agriculture. "Working toward a New Direction in Federal Farm and Food Policy." Press release, n.d. (1994).

Carlson, Gerald A., Carlos Gargiulo, and Biing H. Lin. "The Feed Grain Program Does Not Cause Lower Crop Rotation or Higher Insecticide Use." Unpublished manuscript. North Carolina State University, April 1994.

Coase, Ronald H. "The Problem of Social Cost." *Journal of Law and Economics* 3(1960):1–44.

Cook, Kenneth A., and Andrew B. Art. "Countdown to Compliance: Implementation of the Resource Conservation Requirements of Federal Farm Law." Center for Resource Economics, Washington, D.C., 1993.

Crosson, Pierre. "Cropland and Soils: Past Performance and Policy Challenges." In *America's Renewable Re-*

sources, edited by K.D. Frederick and R.A. Sedjo. Washington, D.C.: Resources for the Future, 1991.

Duffy, Patricia A., and C. Robert Taylor. "The Effects of Increasing Flex Acres on Farm Planning and Profitability." *Agricultural and Resource Economics Review* 23(1994):47–57.

Duffy, Patricia A., C. Robert Taylor, Danny L. Cain, and George J. Young. "The Economic Value of Farm Program Base." *Land Economics* 70(August 1994).

"Ending the Everglades Gridlock." *Sugar y Azucar.* August 1993.

Foster, William E., and Bruce A. Babcock. "Commodity Policy, Price Incentives, and the Growth in Per-Acre Yields." *Journal of Agricultural and Applied Economics* 25(1993):253–65.

———. "The Effects of Government Policy on Flue-cured Tobacco Yields." *Tobacco Science* 34(1990):4–8.

"GAO Says SCS Needs 'Culture Change.'" *Southeast Farm Press,* December 1994, p. 27.

Gardner, B. Delworth. *Plowing Ground in Washington.* San Francisco: Pacific Research Institute, 1995.

Gardner, Bruce. "Causes of U.S. Farm Commodity Programs." *Journal of Political Economy* 95(1987):290–310.

———. *The Impacts of Environmental Protection and Food Safety Regulation on U.S. Agriculture.* Agricultural Policy Working Group, Arlington, Virginia, September 1993.

Gargiulo, Carlos. "Demand for Insecticides in Corn: Effects of Rotations and Government Programs." Ph.D. diss., North Carolina State University, 1992.

Gemmill, Gordon. "An Equilibrium Analysis of U.S. Sugar Policy." *American Journal of Agricultural Economics* 59(1977):609.

———. *The World Sugar Economy: An Econometric Analysis of Production and Policies.* Ph.D. diss., Michigan State University, 1976.

Goodwin, Barry K., and Vincent H. Smith. *The Economics of Crop Insurance and Disaster Aid.* Washington, D.C.: AEI Press, 1995.

Hahn, Robert W. "Saving the Environment and Jobs: A Market-based Approach for Preserving the Everglades." Unpublished manuscript, Economists Incorporated, April 21, 1992.

Helmberger, Peter G. *Economic Analysis of Farm Programs.* New York: McGraw-Hill, 1991.

Johnson, D. Gale. *The Sugar Program: Large Costs and Small Benefits.* Washington, D.C.: American Enterprise Institute, 1974.

LaFrance, Jeffrey T., and Harry de Gorter. "Regulation in a Dynamic Market: The U.S. Dairy Industry." *American Journal of Agricultural Economics* (1985)4:821–32.

Leu, Gwo-Jiun, Andrew Schmitz, and Ronald D. Knutson. "Gains and Losses of Sugar Program Policy Options." *American Journal of Agricultural Economics* 69(1987): 591–602.

Little, D.W. "Sugar Cane Agriculture and the Jamaican Environment." Proceedings from the technical program of the Inter-American Sugar Cane Seminar, 1993.

Lopez, Rigoberto A. "Political Economy of the United States Sugar Policies." *American Journal of Agricultural Economics* 71(1989):20–31.

Lynch, Sarah, and Katherine Reichelderfer Smith. "Lean, Mean and Green: Designing Farm Support Programs in a New Era." Unpublished manuscript, Henry A. Wallace Institute for Alternative Agriculture, Greenbelt, Maryland, November 1994.

Miranowski, John A., and Brian D. Hammes. "Implicit Prices of Soil Characteristics for Farmland in Iowa." *American Journal of Agricultural Economics* 66(1984):745–49.

Miranowski, John A., James Hrubovcak, and John Sutton. "The Effects of Commodity Programs on Resource

Use." In *Commodity and Resource Policy in Agricultural Systems*, edited by R.E. Just and N. Bockstael. New York: Springer-Verlag, 1991.

Moffitt, L. Joe, David Zilberman, and Richard E. Just. "A 'Putty-Clay' Approach to Aggregation of Production/Pollution Possibilities: An Application in Dairy Waste Control." *American Journal of Agricultural Economics* 60(1978):452–59.

Nielsen, E.G., and L.K. Lee. "The Magnitude and Costs of Groundwater Contamination from Agricultural Chemicals: A National Perspective," USDA-ERS, staff report AGES870318, Washington, D.C., 1987.

Osborn, Tim, and Ralph Heimlich. "Changes Ahead for Conservation Reserve Program." *Agricultural Outlook*, July 1994, pp. 26–30.

Pasour, E.C., Jr. *Agriculture and the State: Market Processes and Bureaucracy.* Independent Institute, San Francisco, 1990.

Progressive Farmer, June 1994.

Reichelderfer, Katherine. "Environmental Protection and Agricultural Support: Are Trade-offs Necessary?" In *Agricultural Policies in a New Decade*, edited by Kristen Allen. Washington, D.C.: Resources for the Future and National Planning Association, 1990.

Reichelderfer, Katherine, and William G. Boggess. "Government Decision Making and Program Performance: The Case of the Conservation Program." *American Journal of Agricultural Economics* 70(1988):1–11.

Ribaudo, Marc O. "Program Participation and Chemical Use." Paper presented at the American Agricultural Economics Association meeting, San Diego, California, 1994.

Ruane, J.J., and M.C. Hallberg. "Spatial Equilibrium Analysis for Fluid and Manufacturing Milk in the United States." Pennsylvania Agricultural Experiment Station Bulletin no. 783, June 1986.

Rucker, Randal R., and Walter N. Thurman. "The Economic Effects of Supply Controls: The Simple Analytics of the U.S. Peanut Program." *Journal of Law and Economics* 33(1990):483–515.

Rucker, Randal R., Walter N. Thurman, and Daniel A. Sumner. "Restricting the Market for Quota: An Analysis of Tobacco Production Rights with Corroboration from Congressional Testimony." *Journal of Political Economy* 103(1995):142–75.

Sinner, Jim. "Soil Conservation: We Can Get More for Our Tax Dollars." *Choices* (Second quarter 1990), pp. 10–13.

Smith, Rodney B. "The Conservation Reserve Program as a Least-Cost Land Retirement Mechanism." *American Journal of Agricultural Economics,* forthcoming 1995.

Smith, V. Kerry. "Environmental Costing for Agriculture: Will It Be Standard Fare in the Farm Bill of 2000?" *American Journal of Agricultural Economics* 74(1992):1076–88.

"Soil Erosion Rate Plunges with Compliance in North Carolina." *Carolina Farmer,* June 1994.

Sumner, Daniel A. "Targeting and the Distribution of Program Benefits." In *Agricultural Policies in a New Decade,* edited by Kristen Allen. Washington, D.C.: Resources for the Future and National Planning Association, 1990.

U.S. Department of Agriculture. *Agricultural Statistics,* 1993.

West, D.A., and G.E. Brandow. "Space-Product Equilibrium in the Dairy Industry of the Northeastern and North Central Regions." *Journal of Farm Economics* 46(1964):719–36.

Index

dairy farming, 38–42
externalities concept, 2–4
federal policy instruments,
44, 56
flex acreage effects, 23
geographic distribution of,
58–59
goals of green support programs, 57–58
green support programs,
examples of, 60–64
nonexternal, 5
as policy concerns, 2
policy reform consider-
ations, 67–68
price supports and, 11–13,
24–26
sugar, 34–38
yield-increasing effects of
programs and, 19
Environmental movement
agricultural policy goals,
57–58
interest in agriculture
policy and practice, 1, 49
Environmental reserve concept, 61–62
Erosion
causes, 4
conservation compliance
program, 51–52
Conservation Reserve Pro-
gram, 46, 47–48, 49, 50,
51–52
erodibility index, 51
externalities, 2–3
high-impact crops, 9
nonexternal effects, 50
Externalities
agriculture trends, 3–4
definition, 2–3
price support effects on,
11–13

recipient responsibility, 4–5
response to production
subsidies, 9–10
in soil erosion, 50

Farm labor, 3
Farm practice
acreage diversion in com-
modity programs, 18–20
crop rotation, 21
environmentally sound,
programs to encourage,
60–64
See also Chemical use
Fertilizer
high- and low-demand
crops, 9
runoff effects, 4
in sugar cane farming, 34
Flex acres
effects of, 22
program types, 21–22
role of, 20–21
Food Security Act, 45–47
conservation compliance
provisions, 51–55
swampbuster and sodbus-
ter rules, 55–56
Fraud, 5
Fruit crops, 42

Graduated deficiency pay-
ments, 60–61

Insecticides.
corn, 28
See also Chemical use

Land value
erosivity as factor in, 2n.
supply control programs
and, 31–32
trends, 4

About the Author

WALTER N. THURMAN is a professor in the Department of Agricultural and Resource Economics at North Carolina State University with an appointment in the Economics Department of the same institution. His work on the economic effects of agricultural policy has been published in the *American Journal of Agricultural Economics*, the *Journal of Law and Economics*, and the *Journal of Political Economy*. He has also written on the economics of contracting in agriculture and on the regulation of fisheries.

A NOTE ON THE BOOK

This book was edited by Dana Lane
of the publications staff
of the American Enterprise Institute.
The index was prepared by Robert Elwood.
The text was set in Palatino, a typeface
designed by the twentieth-century Swiss designer
Hermann Zapf. Lisa Roman of the AEI Press
set the type, and Data Reproductions Corporation,
of Rochester Hills, Michigan,
printed and bound the book,
using permanent acid-free paper.

The AEI Press is the publisher for the American Enterprise Institute
for Public Policy Research, 1150 Seventeenth Street, N.W., Washington, D.C. 20036; *Christopher DeMuth*, publisher; *Dana Lane*, director;
Ann Petty, editor; *Leigh Tripoli*, editor; *Cheryl Weissman*, editor; *Lisa
Roman*, editorial assistant (rights and permissions).

www.ingramcontent.com/pod-product-compliance
Lightning Source LLC
Jackson TN
JSHW011941131224
75386JS00041B/1493